LAS VEGAS MADE EASY

ANDY HERBACH
KARL RAAUM

Made Easy
Travel Guides
www.madeeasytravelguides.com

LAS VEGAS MADE EASY
Andy Herbach and Karl Raaum
First Edition © 2024
ISBN: 9798857904817

Acknowledgments
Thanks to our contributors: Megan Raaum,
Erik Raaum, and Erin Raaum
All photos from Karl Raaum, Shutterstock,
Wikimedia Images, and Pixabay

ABOUT THE AUTHORS

Andy Herbach is the author of the *Eating & Drinking* series of menu translators and restaurant guides, including *Eating & Drinking in Paris, Eating & Drinking in Italy, Eating & Drinking in Spain and Portugal, Eating & Drinking in Germany,* and *Eating & Drinking in Latin America.* He is also the author of *Paris Walks, Unique Paris, Wining & Dining in Paris, Wining & Dining in Italy, Europe Made Easy, Paris Made Easy, Amsterdam Made Easy, Berlin Made Easy, Barcelona Made Easy, Madrid and Toledo Made Easy, Nice and the French Riviera Made Easy, Oslo Made Easy, Provence Made Easy, Wales Made Easy, Palm Springs Made Easy, San Diego Made Easy, Southern California Made Easy, Las Vegas Made Easy,* and *The Amazing California Desert.* **Karl Raaum** has contributed to all the *Made Easy* travel guides and is the co-author of *Wining & Dining in Paris, Wining & Dining in Italy, Palm Springs Made Easy, San Diego Made Easy, Southern California Made Easy, Las Vegas Made Easy,* and *The Amazing California Desert.* The authors live in Palm Springs, California.

You can e-mail corrections, additions, and comments to
eatndrink@aol.com or through
www.madeeasytravelguides.com.

TABLE OF CONTENTS

1. **Introduction** 9
2. **Las Vegas Sights** 11
3. **Excursions** 67
    Spring Mountains National Recreation Area/Mount Charleston 69
    Red Rock Canyon 70
    Valley of Fire 72
    Death Valley 74
    Mojave National Preserve 83
    Primm 86
    Laughlin 87
    Hoover Dam and Lake Mead 88
    Grand Canyon (West Rim) 89
    Pahrump 90
4. **Sleeping & Eating** 91
    Sleeping 91
    Shows 100
    Eating 103
5. **Planning Your Trip/Practical Matters** 109
6. **Index** 116

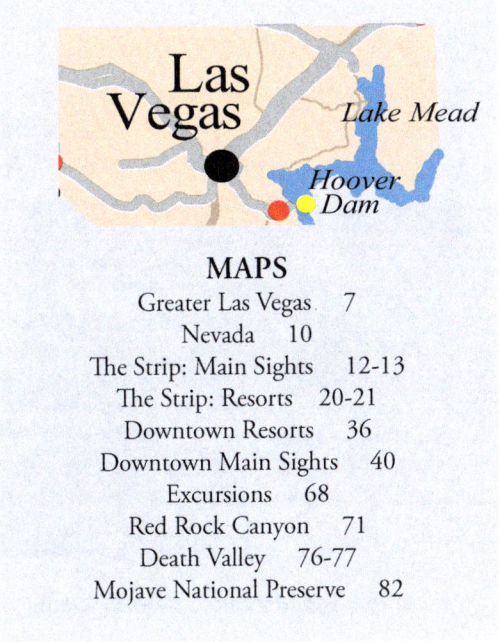

MAPS
Greater Las Vegas 7
Nevada 10
The Strip: Main Sights 12-13
The Strip: Resorts 20-21
Downtown Resorts 36
Downtown Main Sights 40
Excursions 68
Red Rock Canyon 71
Death Valley 76-77
Mojave National Preserve 82

4

Part with your money at one of many the casinos.

Explore the incredible Hoover Dam.

Walk along Las Vegas Boulevard ("The Strip").

Take a day trip to scenic Death Valley.

Hike or take a scenic drive through Red Rock Canyon.

Escape the summer heat by floating in a pool!

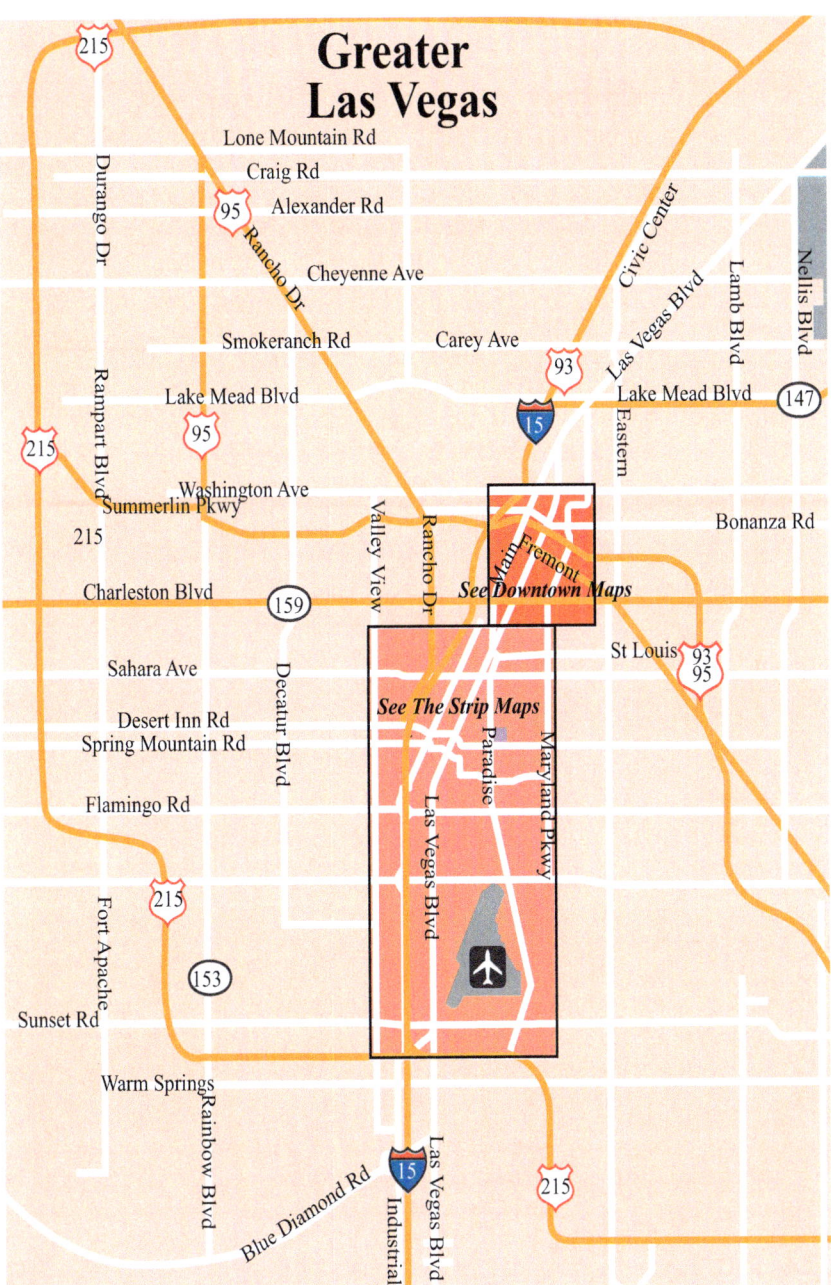

REVIEWS OF OUR TRAVEL GUIDES

•

"..an opinionated little compendium."
Eating & Drinking in Paris
~ New York Times

"Everything you need to devour Paris on the quick."
Best of Paris
~ Chicago Tribune

"an elegant, small guide..."
Eating & Drinking in Italy
~ Minneapolis Star Tribune

"Makes dining easy and enjoyable."
Eating & Drinking in Spain
~ Toronto Sun

"Guide illuminates the City of Light."
Wining & Dining in Paris
~ Newsday

"This handy pocket guide is all you need..."
Paris Made Easy
~ France Magazine

"Small enough for discreet use..."
Eating & Drinking in Paris
~ USA Today

"It's written as if a friend were talking to you."
Eating & Drinking in Italy
~ Celebrity Chef Tyler Florence

1. INTRODUCTION

Las Vegas is flashy, fun, and fabulous! There's something for everyone in this oasis in the desert. A slot machine is practically everywhere you turn if you want to gamble (from the airport to gas stations). If you want to be entertained, the city hosts some of the most popular performers in residence. Feeling naughty, well...

There's so much more to Nevada's largest city. Fascinating sights and museums include the Neon Museum, Mob Museum, and the incredible Sphere. You can take an excursion to the massive Hoover Dam, the majestic Grand Canyon, the blazing hot Death Valley, and the stark Mojave Desert.

We'll explore exciting nightlife and resorts, including insider tips on restaurants and shops. This pocket guide will help you plan your trip with confidence. However short your stay, it's all you'll need to make your visit enjoyable, memorable—and easy!

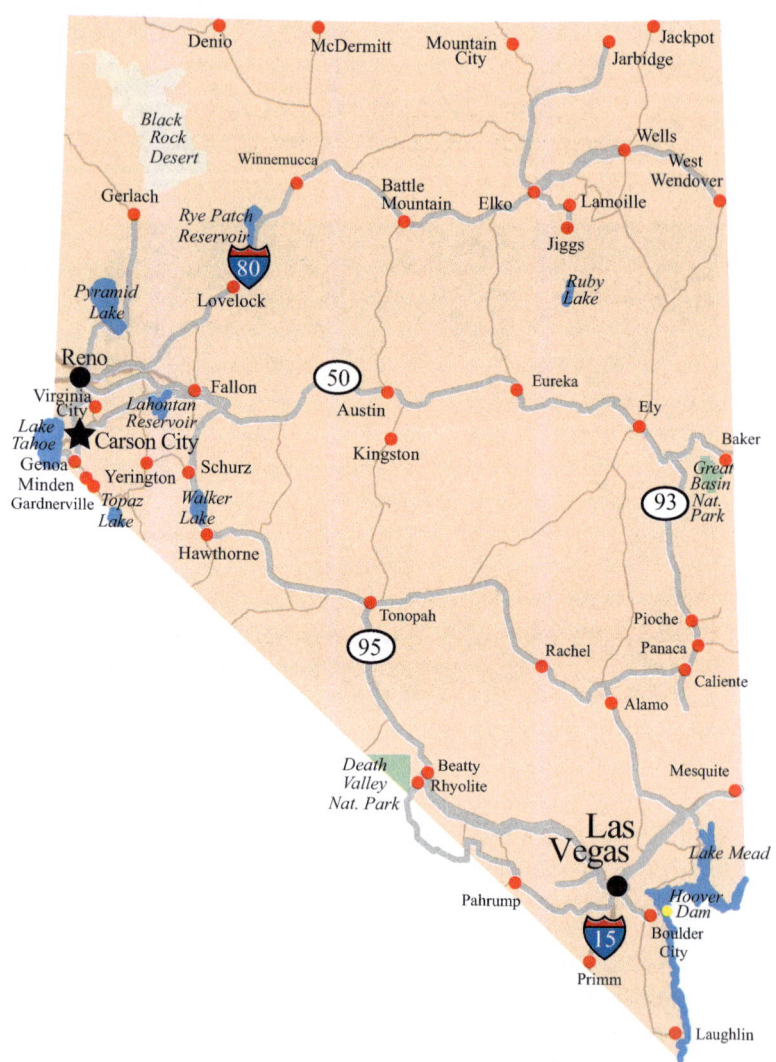

THINGS CHANGE!

Phone numbers, prices, addresses, and quality of food all change. It would be wise to check websites for updated information before your visit. It's advisable to book online for entrance to many of the most popular sights. Some even allow you to schedule your visit for a specific entry time.

2. Las Vegas Sights

- The Strip
- Rat Pack
- Downtown
- Wedding Chapels
- Further Afield
- Sports Teams
- Las Vegas for Kids
- A History of Gambling in Las Vegas
- The LGBTQ+ Scene
- Shopping
- Pool Scene
- Golfing

12 LAS VEGAS MADE EASY

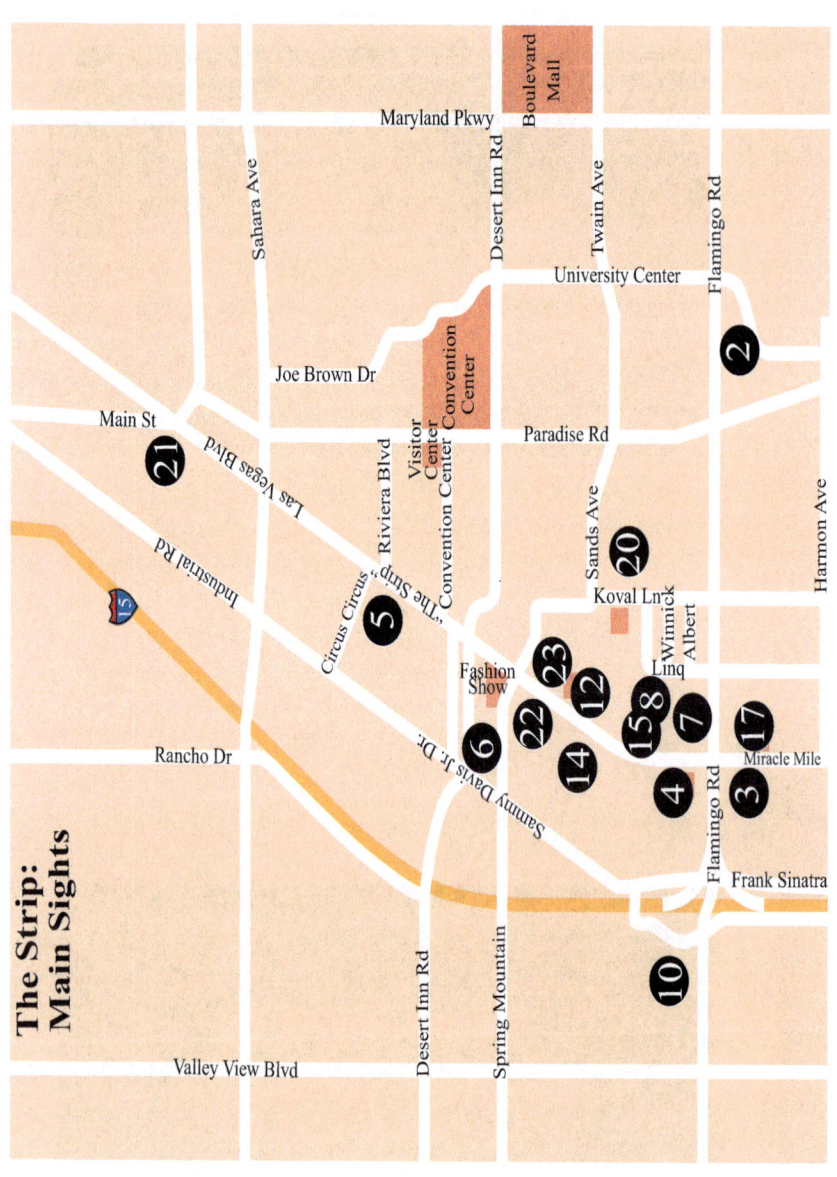

LAS VEGAS SIGHTS 13

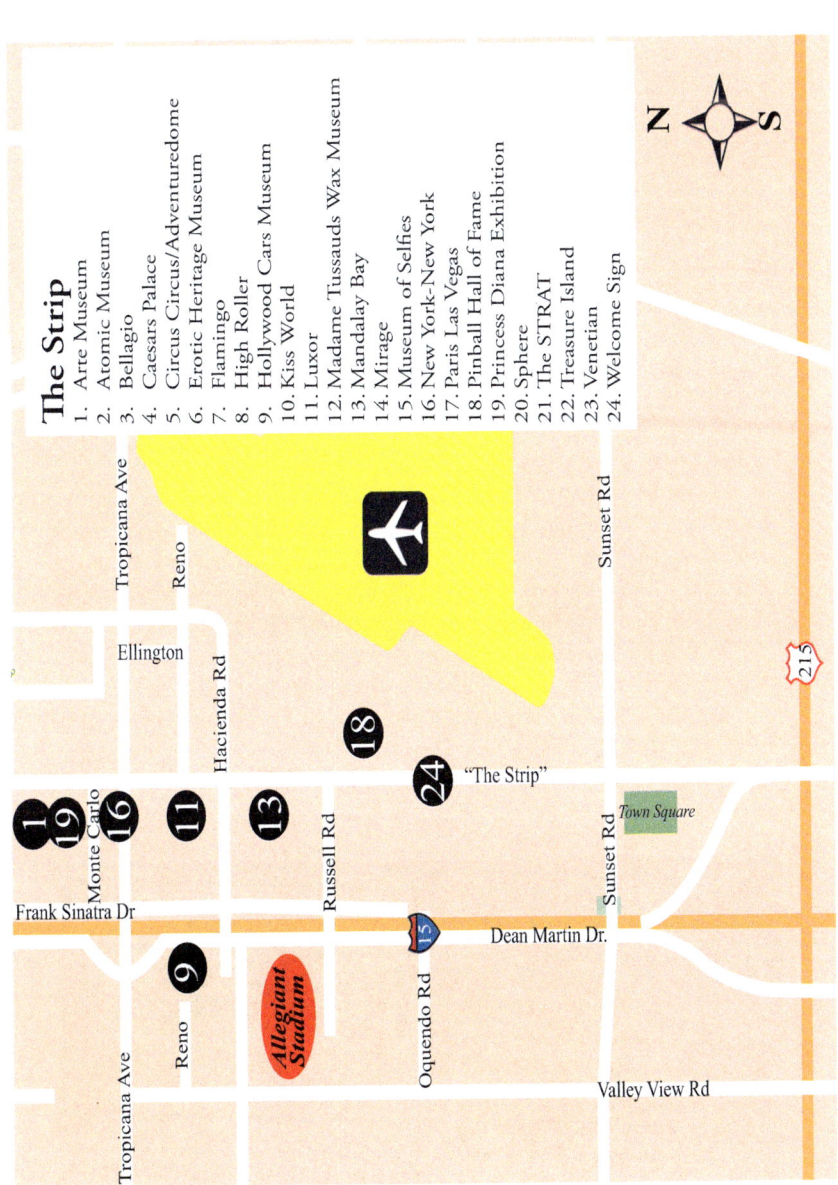

THE STRIP

When you think of Las Vegas, you most likely picture "The Strip." No trip to the city would be complete without a walk down this section of Las Vegas Boulevard. The Strip is lined with enormous theme resorts, entertainment venues, and dining for every budget. It's impressive at night, when The Strip shines with one glittering neon sign after another. According to NASA, The Strip is the world's brightest area, thanks to its concentrated display of lights. Some of the massive hotels and casinos along The Strip include Luxor, Cosmopolitan, Venetian, Bellagio, STRAT, Circus Circus, New York-New York, Mandalay Bay, Treasure Island, MGM, Paris Las Vegas, and Caesars Palace. *Info*: South Las Vegas Boulevard. See the main sights maps on pages 12-13 and the resorts maps on pages 20-21.

LAS VEGAS SIGHTS 15

The Welcome to Fabulous Las Vegas Sign
The Welcome to Fabulous Las Vegas sign is at the southern end of The Strip. The iconic retro sign was erected in 1959. Neon artist Betty Willis designed the sign, and it remains a popular landmark. You'll find visitors taking photos and posing 24 hours a day! *Info*: 5100 S. Las Vegas Blvd.

Another welcome marker is on The Strip between St. Louis Avenue and Bob Stupak Avenue at the base of The STRAT Hotel and Casino. Illuminated 80-foot-tall arches frame a Las Vegas welcome sign.

16 LAS VEGAS MADE EASY

Nearby at 1810 South Las Vegas Boulevard is the "Showgirl Sign" featuring 50-foot-tall showgirls. The popular sight for selfies lights up day and night. *Info*: On the corner of Main Street and South Las Vegas Boulevard.

The Pyramid at Luxor
Among all the splashy resorts in Las Vegas, this hotel in the shape of a pyramid, is one of the most recognizable. You can visit New York City at the New York-New York resort and Italy at the Venetian and Bellagio resorts, and you can take in Egypt at the Luxor. At 350 feet (107 meters) tall, the pyramid at the Luxor is almost as large as the ancient pyramids in Egypt. It's massive, with 30 stories, 4,400 guest rooms, casino, restaurants,

spa, entertainment venues, and an enormous 19,000 square-foot pool. With an ancient Egyptian theme, the Luxor boasts the world's largest atrium. The tip of the pyramid has a light beam, which is said to be the most powerful man-made light in the world. The best time to visit is at night when the pyramid is illuminated. *Info*: 3900 S. Las Vegas Blvd. luxor.mgmresorts.com.

Titanic: The Artifact Exhibition
Artifacts from the Titanic wreck site are on display at the Luxor. You're given a replica of a boarding pass, of the ill-fated cruise ship, to begin your exploration. The 25,000-square-foot exhibit features over 350 items recovered over 2.5 miles (4 km) beneath the surface of the Atlantic Ocean. You'll see window frames, pots, pans, luggage, champagne bottles, and a 15-ton piece of the ship's hull, recovered from the 1912 disaster. Rooms of the ship have been reconstructed, including a full-size replica of the ship's Grand Staircase. *Info*: 3900. S Las Vegas Blvd. Tel. 800/557-7428. Admission: $32, ages 4-12 $25. www.titaniclasvegas.com.

Bodies...The Exhibition
Another exhibit at the Luxor is this fascinating exploration of the human body. Using an innovative preservation process, 13 human bodies and over 260 organs and body parts are displayed. An interesting part of the exhibit is the portrayal of health issues such as smoking, obesity, and alcohol use. For example, visitors can compare a healthy lung with one that has been ravaged by smoking. Some controversy has surrounded the exhibit

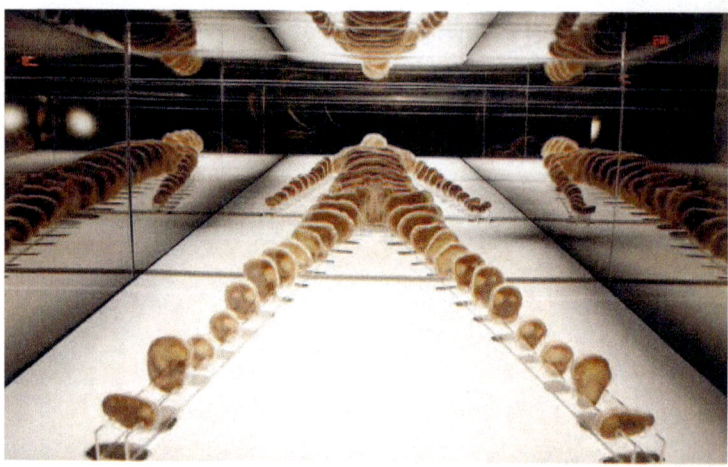

as human rights groups have raised concerns that the bodies are those of executed Chinese prisoners, and that the families of the victims have not given consent or received compensation for their display. *Info*: 3900. S Las Vegas Blvd.. Tel. 800/557-7428. Open daily 11am-6pm. Admission: $32. Combined admission with the Titanic: The Artifact Exposition (also at Luxor) is $42.00. bodieslasvegas.com.

Cirque du Soleil at Treasure Island
The enormous Treasure Island Resort on The Strip has been home to *Mystère* by Cirque du Soleil for over three decades. The show combines music, lights, dance, and incredible acrobatic numbers. There are 90-minute performances two times a night, five nights a week. *Info*: 3300 S. Las Vegas Blvd. Tel. 877/773-6470. Shows Fri-Tue at 7pm and 9:30pm. Admission: From $42. www.cirquedusoleil.com.

LAS VEGAS SIGHTS 19

The Sphere
This enormous, new entertainment venue is the world's largest spherical structure at 366 feet (111 meters) tall and 516 feet (157 meters) wide. It cost $2.3 billion to construct. It glows, day and night, with over a million lights. The bowl-shaped theater houses the world's highest-resolution wrap-around LED screen. If you attend an event here, the venue seats 18,000 people and your experience is enhanced by the 250-feet-tall (76 meters) screen that wraps around the venue. A splashy addition to the city's skyline. *Info*: 255 Sands Avenue (a block east of The Strip and east of the Venetian resort). Tel. 725/258-6724. www.thespherevegas.com.

High Roller
If you really want to take in the views of The Strip, you can soar 550 feet (168 meters) riding the largest observation wheel in North America. The Ferris wheel takes 30 minutes to complete one revolution. There are 28 spacious cabins. *Info*: 3545 S. Las Vegas Blvd. Tel. 855/234-7469. Open daily noon-midnight. Admission: From $23.50. www.caesars.com/linq/things-to-do/attractions/high-roller.

20 LAS VEGAS MADE EASY

LAS VEGAS SIGHTS 21

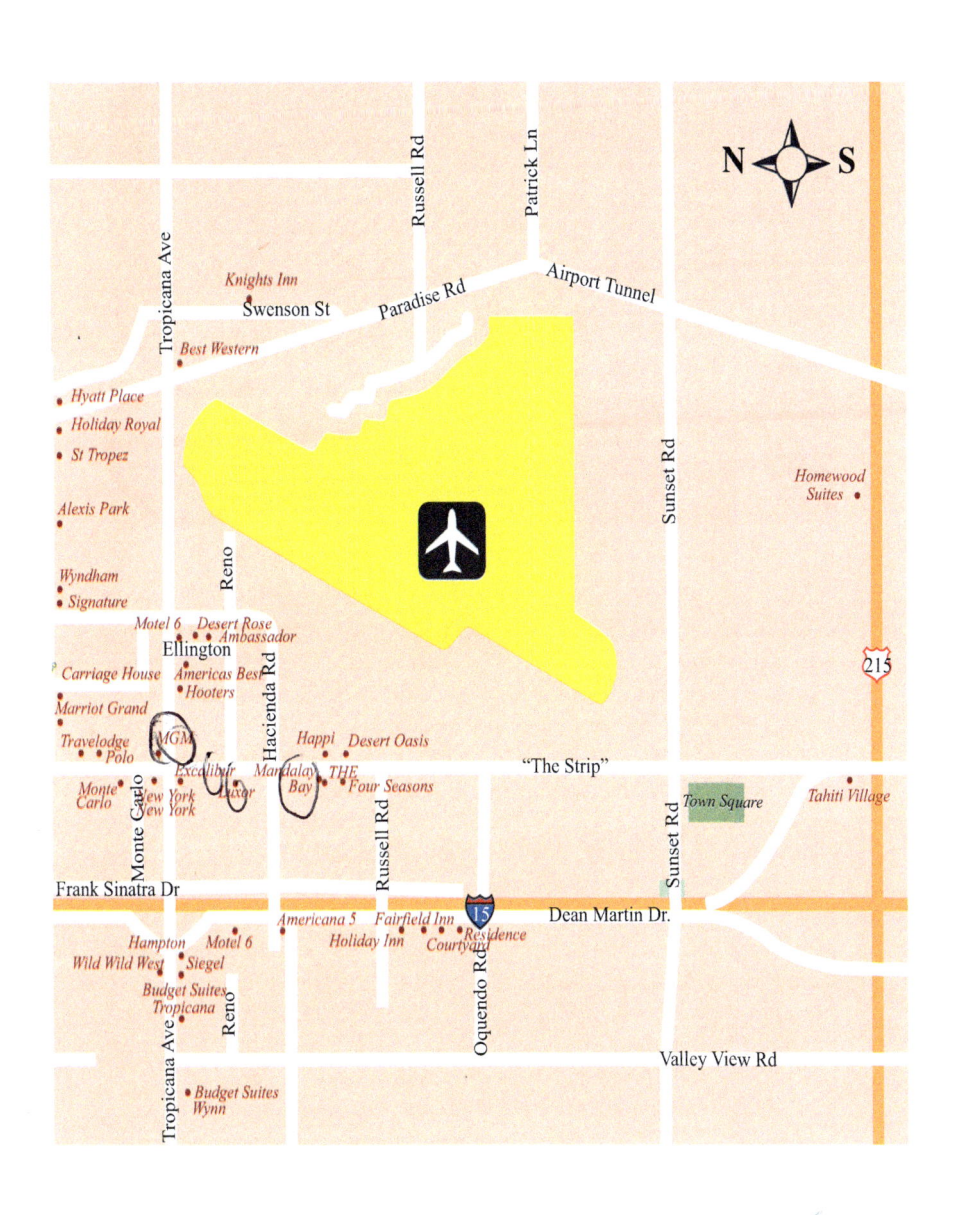

Fountains of Bellagio
You can view this free attraction from the sidewalk along The Strip in front of the Bellagio Hotel. The massive fountain is inside a man-made lake that is modeled after Lake Como in Italy. Waterworks are synchronized with a changing playlist and light show, so you'll likely never see the same show twice. The playlist features everything from light opera to current pop songs. Water shoots as high as 460 feet (140 meters), has 1,200 nozzles to spray in different directions, and there are nearly 4,800 color lights to illuminate the fountain. *Info*: Bellagio Hotel at 3600 S. Las Vegas Blvd. Shows are every half-hour from the afternoon to midnight. Admission: Free.

Bellagio Conservatory & Botanical Gardens
Besides the Bellagio fountains, inside the resort you'll find the magnificent Conservatory & Botanical Gardens. The 14,000-square-foot green space is transformed five times a year using and reusing rare plants from throughout the world. It's an explosion of color and scents. The yearly themes include Lunar New Year (mid-January to early March), spring (early March to mid-May), summer (late May to early September), harvest/autumn (mid-September to early November), and winter/holidays (mid-November to early January). *Info*: Bellagio Hotel at 3600 S. Las Vegas Blvd. Open 24 hours. Admission: Free.

LAS VEGAS SIGHTS 23

STRAT Tower
Soaring 1,149 feet (350 meters) above The Strip, this is the tallest observation tower in the country. Floor-to-ceiling windows allow you to enjoy incredible views of Las Vegas from the indoor and outdoor observation deck or have a drink or meal at the bar and restaurant. *Info*: 2000 Las Vegas Blvd. South. Tel. 800/998-6937. Open daily 10am-1am. Admission: $20. www.thestrat.com. Feeling brave? Then try **SkyJump**, a combination of bungee jumping and skydiving. You'll be strapped into a harness, then jump off the tower reaching speeds of up to 40 miles (64 km) per hour. From $149.99. Reservations required at tickets.thestrat.com.

Gondola Rides at the Venetian Resort
The Venetian Resort attempts to replicate the sights of Venice, including the Grand Canal, Rialto Bridge, St. Mark's Square, and the Doge's Palace. One of the unique experiences is taking an outdoor or indoor gondola ride. Inside, you'll pass under bridges of the cobblestone streets of the **Grand Canal Shoppes**. The outdoor trip offers views of reproductions of the sights of Venice and of The Strip. Choose between a private two-person gondola or a four-person shared ride. The trip lasts 15 minutes. Singing gondoliers guide you through the canals. Dorky? You decide. *Info*: 3355 S. Las Vegas Blvd. Indoor: Emporio di Gondola Level 2, Grand Canal Shoppes. Outdoor: Gondola Ticket Booth, Doge's Palace. Tel. 702/414-4300. Outdoor: daily 10am-10pm. Indoor: Mon-Thu and Sun 10am-11pm, Fri and Sat 10am-midnight. Admission: From $34 per person. www.venetianlasvegas.com/resort/attractions/gondola-rides.html.

Adventuredome at Circus Circus
This indoor amusement park is in the Circus Circus Resort and Casino. Circus Circus is the largest permanent big top in the world. It's meant to combine a circus, carnival, and fair under one roof. It's free to wander around, but most purchase an all-day pass. The five-acre space includes rides and attractions, including the Canyon Blaster, the world's only indoor double-loop, double-corkscrew roller coaster. Some attractions include miniature golf, midway games, video arcade, bumper cars, rock climbing, bungee jumping, virtual reality room, and clown shows. *Info*: 2800 S. Las Vegas Blvd. Tel. 702/794-3939. Open daily at 10am. Admission: $60 (all-day pass for adults), $30 (children under four feet). www.circuscircus.com.

Paris Las Vegas and the Eiffel Tower Experience
You won't see the Champs-Élysées or the Paris skyline, but you will be rewarded with fantastic views of Las Vegas from this observation deck. The Eiffel Tower of Vegas is half the size of the real one in France. You'll be 46 stories above the city's skyline. If you want to dine on French cuisine, the Eiffel Tower Restaurant is here, too. *Info*: 3655 S. Las Vegas Blvd. Tel. 888/727-4758. Open daily noon-midnight. Admission: From $24.50. www.caesars.com/paris-las-vegas/things-to-do/eiffel-tower.

LAS VEGAS SIGHTS 25

Shark Reef Aquarium at Mandalay Bay Resort
Shark Reef Aquarium at the Mandalay Bay Resort has over 2,000 species of aquatic life, including sharks, giant rays, sea turtles, piranhas, and exotic fish. You can walk through a shark tunnel and take in the endangered and threatened marine species in the Shipwreck Tank. If you'd like to experience swimming with a humpback whale or along sharks, you can put on a headset at the Virtual Reality Theater. Additional experiences (at additional cost) include a Stingray Feed and Shark Feed. *Info*: 3950 S. Las Vegas Blvd. Tel. 702.632.4555. Open daily 10am-8pm. Admission: From $29. mandalaybay.mgmresorts.com/en/entertainment/shark-reef-aquarium.html.

Atomic Museum
This museum, an affiliate of the Smithsonian Institution, covers the history of nuclear testing at the Nevada Test Site (NTS) in the desert northwest of Las Vegas. The focus is on the first test in Nevada on January 27, 1951. The exhibit delves into the "Atomic Age," which began during World War II and continued until the declaration of a worldwide ban on nuclear testing in 1992. Exhibits include Geiger counters and radiation testing devices. "Ground Zero Theater" simulates the scary experience of a nuclear test. On a lighter side, the exhibition displays pop culture memorabilia, including everything from toys, television shows, and comic books. The ticket booth is a replica of a Nevada Test Site guard station. One particularly poignant exhibit examines the environmental legacy of atomic testing and its impact on Native American lands. *Info*: 755 E. Flamingo Rd. Tel. 702/409-7366. Open daily 9am-5pm. Admission: $29. www.atomicmuseum.vegas.

Big Apple Coaster at New York-New York
You're not on Coney Island, but you can pretend you are on this roller coaster at the New York-New York Resort. Among the replicas of the skyscrapers, Statue of Liberty, and Brooklyn Bridge, you'll find this coaster that has speeds that reach up to 67 miles (108 km) per hour. At one point, there's a 203 foot (62 meter) drop! You must be at least 54 inches tall to ride. There's also a large game arcade. *Info*: 3790 S. Las Vegas Blvd. Tel. 702/740-6616. Open Mon-Thu 11am-11pm, Fri-Sun 11am-midnight. Admission: $25. newyorknewyork.mgmresorts.com

Arte Museum
The immersive art experience spreads over two floors and 30,000 square feet. Each area of the museum places the visitor among the elements of nature. All five senses are engaged. You'll be at the base of waterfalls, find yourself surrounded by and smelling blooming flowers, and exploring the forest. One exhibit allows you to draw an animal, have it scanned, and watch your creation come to life on the screen. An interesting interactive museum. Note that the entrance price is not cheap. *Info*: 3716 S. Las Vegas Blvd., Suite 208. Tel. 702/725-7200. Open daily 10am-11pm. Admission: From $55. lasvegas.artemuseum.com.

Madame Tussauds Wax Museum
If you want to take a selfie with your favorite stars of music, film, or sports, this is the place to come. Over 100 lifelike wax figures are here, including Miley Cyrus, Beyoncé, Jennifer Aniston, and Elvis Presley. There are also sections with historical figures and Marvel Superheroes. The Marvel Universe is a 4D experience with characters from Black Panther to Captain America. *Info*: 3377 S. Las Vegas Blvd. Tel. 702/862-7800. Open daily 10am-8pm. Admission: From $38.99. www.madametussauds.com/las vegas.

Shopping at The Forum Shops at Caesars
Las Vegas isn't just about spending your money on gambling and entertainment. It's also known for the wide array of shopping options. On The Strip, connected to the Caesars Palace Resort, is this shopping mall with over 160 stores and restaurants. You'll find everything from Armani to Levi's. A popular, and free, attraction here is **The Atlantis Show**, with nine-foot-tall talking statues that come to life (animatronic statues) to tell the story of the ill-fated city of Atlantis. Fountains, fire, lasers, steam, and sound effects add to the display. From Thursday to Monday, the show is usually played on the hour, from noon to 8pm. Nearby is a 50,000-gallon **aquarium** filled with over 300 saltwater fish. *Info*: Inside Caesars Palace Forum Shops at the intersection of The Strip and Flamingo Road. Admission: Free. www.simon.com/mall/the-forum-shops-at-caesars-palace.

Escape Game Las Vegas is also at The Forum Shops. Each game has multiple rooms to explore. You can choose from a variety of themes and difficulties, including Prison Break, The Depths, The Heist, Mysterious Market, Gold Rush, and Search For Lost Toys. *Info*: Inside Caesars Palace Forum Shops at the intersection of The Strip and Flamingo Road. Tel. 702/710-8144. Open daily 8am-midnight. Admission: From $42. www.theescapegame.com/lasvegas.

Pinball Hall of Fame

Across from the iconic "Welcome To Fabulous Las Vegas" sign (*see page 15*) is this museum dedicated to pinball. Over 1,000 classic pinball and video games are on display, spread over 25,000-square-feet. Most of the games are from the 1960s through 1980s, the heyday of pinball. There's Wheel of Fortune, Donkey Kong, and Pac-Man, just to name a few. The museum is maintained by the Las Vegas Pinball Collectors Club, a non-profit organization. It's the world's largest collection of functioning pinball machines. All the games are playable, so bring some coins! There are money changing machines if you only have paper money. *Info*: 4925 S. Las Vegas Blvd. Tel. 702/597-2627. Open daily 10am-9pm (Fri and Sat until 10pm). Admission: Free. www.pinballmuseum.org.

Erotic Heritage Museum

It's appropriate that the largest erotic museum in the world is in "Sin City." The interactive exhibits rotate frequently. Adult films play on screens throughout the museum. There's an exhibit of the history of the adult film industry and features some of the "biggest" adult film stars through the ages. Erotic artifacts on display date back to 1,500 BCE. The museum has a live show "Puppetry of the Penis." Grab a drink (there's a bar) and make sure you check out the fun souvenirs in the gift shop. You must be 18 years or older to enter. *Info*: 3275 Sammy Davis Jr. Dr. Tel. 702/794-4000. Open Mon-Wed 11am-7pm, Thu-Sun 11am-10pm. Admission: $29. www.eroticmuseumvegas.com.

LAS VEGAS SIGHTS 29

Hollywood Cars Museum
Does that vehicle look familiar? If it does, it's probably because you have seen it on the big screen or television. Some of the film's most famous cars are on display at this museum. In the **Liberace Garage**, you'll see his glittery vehicles, including a red, white, and blue "Bicentennial" Rolls Royce. Our favorite is the 40-foot pink hot tub convertible limo, seen on the television show *Lifestyles of the Rich and Famous*. Some of the notable cars at the museum include:
- Five James Bond vehicles, including the Lotus Esprit Submarine Car driven in the film, *The Spy Who Loved Me*
- Batmobile from the *Batman* movie
- Delorean from *Back to the Future*
- Herbie from *Love Bug*
- Several vehicles from *Fast and Furious*
- Grand Torino from *Starsky and Hutch*
- Coffin Dragster "Drag-u-La" from *The Munsters*

Info: 5115 Dean Martin Dr. Tel. 702/331-6400. Open daily 10am-5pm. Admission: $20. Cash only. Under age 16 free with paid adult admission. Discount coupon on its website. hollywoodcarsmuseum.com.

KISS World Mini Golf and Museum
The rock group KISS is the theme at this indoor 18-hole mini golf course at the Rio Hotel and Casino. You'll listen to a playlist of KISS songs while playing on a glow-in-the-dark course. There are arcade games, rock 'n roll gift shop, and even a wedding chapel (with ceremonies officiated by a Gene Simmons impersonator). The memorabilia includes gold and platinum records, Rock and Roll Hall of Fame award, costumes, and album covers. A must for KISS fans. *Info*: 3700 W. Flamingo Rd. Tel. 702/558-6256. Open daily noon-10pm (Fri and Sat until 11pm). Admission: $12.95. www.kissminigolf.com.

Wildlife Habitat at the Flamingo
This Las Vegas institution, with its iconic pink exterior, opened in 1946. It's one of the oldest resorts on The Strip. Mobster Bugsy Siegel built the hotel and casino, and he was murdered after it opened. It has seen expansion and renovation over the years and now has over 3,500 guest rooms. Featured performers have included Rat Pack members Frank Sinatra, Dean Martin, and Sammy Davis Jr. The highlight is Wildlife Habitat, where you can roam four acres of gardens with waterfalls, winding streams, fish, exotic birds, and, of course, flamingos. *Info*: 3555 S. Las Vegas Blvd. Open daily 7am-8pm. Admission: Free. www.caesars.com/flamingo-las-vegas/things-to-do/wildlife-habitat.

Museum of Selfies
If you think your selfies are boring, check out this do-it-yourself photography studio and selfie museum. You'll have an hour to take as many photos and videos that you want. There are over 20 backgrounds available. Some of the fun sets include:
- **Private Jet**: Pretend you're on a private jet and drinking champagne.
- **Twinkling Lights**: Pose in a room of multi-colored hanging lights.
- **Tub of Gold**: Relax in a bathtub of gold.
- **Ball Pit**: Get buried in yellow emoji squishy balls.
- **Sideways Room**: Look as though you're levitating over a bed, hanging from a door handle, climbing the walls, and standing upside down.
- **Food**: Photograph yourself with giant food.

Info: LINQ Promenade, 3545 S. Las Vegas Blvd. Tel. 702/518-2277. Open daily 10am-midnight. Admission: $30. selfievegas.com.

LAS VEGAS SIGHTS 31

Princess Diana: A Tribute Exhibition
Take a journey through 12 theme rooms that tell the life story of Princess Diana. A collection of royal memorabilia, one of the most comprehensive in the world, displays her designer clothes and personal effects. The theme rooms include "The White House and the Palace," "Wedding of the Century," and "Fashion Icon." You'll see the largest collection of authentic evening gowns worn by the late princess. There are over 700 artifacts from not only Diana, but King Charles, the late Queen Elizabeth II, Prince William, and Prince Harry. *Info*: 3720 S. Las Vegas Blvd. The Shops at Crystals Third Floor/Aria Resort. Tel. 702/590-9299. Open daily 10am-6pm. Admission: $32.85 (online purchase). dianalasvegas.com.

The Mirage Volcano
This popular free attraction has been entertaining visitors and locals since 1989. In front of the Mirage Hotel and Casino, you'll find a volcano that explodes into flames, with eruptions of water, and a choreographed soundtrack. The same group that designed the fabulous fountains at the Bellagio designed this attraction. *Info*: 3400 S. Las Vegas Blvd. Shows daily at 8pm, 9pm, 10pm, and 11pm. Admission: Free. www.hardrockhotelcasinolasvegas.com/amenities/volcano.

RAT PACK

The Rat Pack was a group of famous entertainers that included Frank Sinatra, Dean Martin, Peter Lawford, Sammy Davis Jr., and Joey Bishop. Shirley MacLaine, Marilyn Monroe, and Angie Dickinson were often referred to as the "Rat Pack Mascots." Some of them even appeared together in films such as *Ocean's 11*, *Robin and the 7 Hoods*, and *Some Came Running*. In the late 1950s and 1960s, the Rat Pack spent much of their time in Las Vegas.

At the height of their popularity, in the first half of the 1960s, fans flocked to the Sands Hotel and Casino in Las Vegas to see the Rat Pack perform. They demolished the Sands, but here are a few of the Rat Pack hangouts that remain.

Golden Steer

Want to eat at the same table where Frank Sinatra drank a martini and dined? This steakhouse, open since 1958, offers "the best steak on earth." We're not sure about that, but at least you can feel the same vibe as Sammy Davis Jr. did. Oh, Elvis dined here, too. *Info*: 308 W. Sahara Ave. www.goldensteerlasvegas.com.

LAS VEGAS SIGHTS

Atomic Liquors
Opened in 1952, this is the oldest free-standing bar in Las Vegas. Movies like *The Hangover* and *Casino* have featured this downtown bar. The Rat Pack cavorted here (and so did Barbra Streisand). *Info*: 917 E Fremont St. www.atomic.vegas.

Caesars Palace
Frank Sinatra began performing at the theater here in 1967. Back in the day, you could see him gambling at the hotel's casino and drinking with Dean Martin at Cleopatra's Barge Lounge (which has now closed). *Info*: 3570 S. Las Vegas Blvd. www.caesars.com.

Golden Gate Hotel
Golden Gate Hotel, which opened downtown in 1906, is one of the oldest casinos in Las Vegas. It's an original hangout of the Rat Pack. *Info*: 1 Fremont St. www.goldengatecasino.com.

Peppermill Restaurant and Fireside Lounge
Featured in the films *Showgirls* and *Casino*, this restaurant and bar opened in 1972. Rat Pack members, especially Dean Martin, Jerry Lewis, and Joey Bishop, drank many tiki cocktails here, under its neon lights. *Info*: 2985 S. Las Vegas Blvd. www.peppermilllasvegas.com.

DOWNTOWN

While most think that The Strip is the heart of Las Vegas, downtown is the historic heart of the city. Fremont Street Experience is a mall with shops, light shows, and the SlotZilla zip line. The fabulous Neon Museum, home to historic neon signs, is here. You can also check out the history of mobs in Nevada at the Mob Museum, head to the cultural hub of the city at The Arts District, get creepy at Zak Bagans' Haunted Museum, and pawn your stuff at the Gold and Silver Pawn Shop. The kids will enjoy Discovery Children's Museum and the Las Vegas Natural History Museum. Hungry or thirsty? Dining options and bars range from casual to fancy. There is truly something for everyone in downtown Las Vegas! *Info*: The main street of downtown is along Fremont Street. See the downtown resorts map on page 36 and the downtown sights map on page 40 and 41.

Neon Museum

Las Vegas is known for its glitzy neon signs, and this downtown museum is where old neon signs go when they're no longer needed. The 2.25-acre campus includes the outdoor space known as the Neon Boneyard, the home of over 250 signs (dating back to the 1930s), many of which have been restored. The visitors' center is housed inside the former La Concha Motel lobby. Among the signs featured here are the original Horseshoe and Stardust signs. Although you can visit during the day, it's best to experience the museum at night when many of the signs are illuminated. Guided tours are about one hour and you'll learn much about old Las Vegas. Also here is the laser-light show "Brilliant" set to music. *Info*: 770 Las Vegas Blvd. Tel. 702/387-6366. Open daily Mar-Apr and Sep-Oct 3pm-11pm, May-Aug 4pm-midnight, Nov-Feb 2pm-10pm. Admission: From $20. Advanced reservations through the website. www.neonmuseum.org.

36 LAS VEGAS MADE EASY

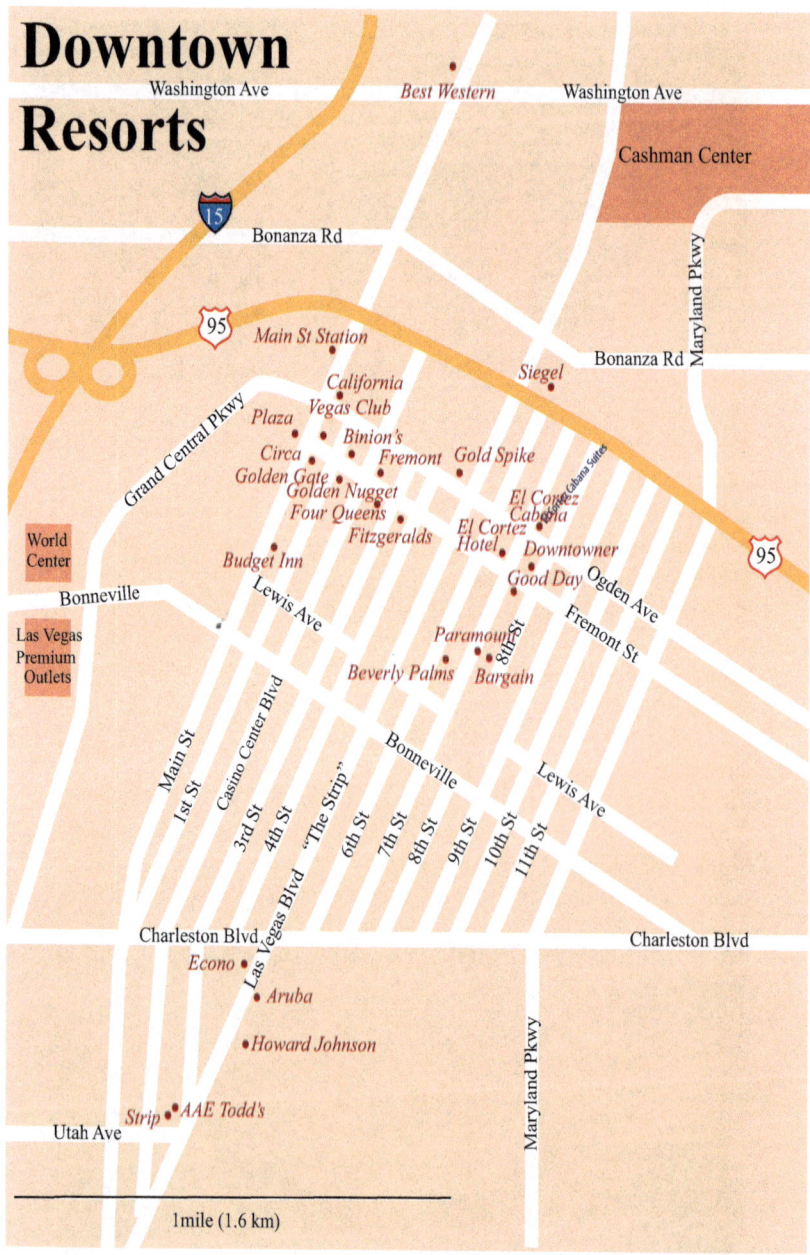

LAS VEGAS SIGHTS

Fremont Street Experience
Before massive resorts and casinos, there was Fremont Street. Located north of The Strip, this area was the center of the city and known as "Glitter Gulch." The city's iconic original neon marquees and signs included the Golden Nugget, Pioneer Club, Binion's Horseshoe, and Vegas Vickie kicking her booted leg into the air.

Today, it's an expansive, pedestrian only, outdoor mall with 10 casinos, live entertainment, open-air bars, restaurants for every budget, zip line (*see below*), and the Neon and Mob museums. Also here is the Viva Vision canopy (*see photo below*), the largest LED canopy screen in the world with over 16 million brilliant pixels. It's suspended 90 feet (27.4 meters) above the pedestrian mall. *Info*: North of The Strip in downtown along Fremont Street. Admission: Free. vegasexperience.com.

SlotZilla is a slot machine-inspired zip line offering two lines. The lower "Zip-Zilla" is seven stories up ($49) and the upper "Super Hero Zoom" is eleven stories up ($69). The lower line travels halfway down the Fremont Street Experience pedestrian mall and the upper line goes the entire length of the mall (1,750 feet/533 meters).

The Arts District (18b)
Want to get away from gambling, neon lights, and tourists? Head to "18b," named for this 18-block zone southwest of downtown. This cultural hub features art galleries, boutiques, cafes, restaurants, and bars. Don't forget that Las Vegas isn't just a bunch of tourists, but a vibrant and large city with a youthful population, and this is where they head. The Antique Alley Mall has over 20 antique and vintage shops. Stores like Retro Vegas feature mid-century modern fare, especially from old casinos. Also here is the Cockroach Theatre staging plays and revivals. This is real Vegas. *Info*: Between the Fremont Street Experience and the STRAT Resort, around Main Street and Charleston Boulevard. www.18barts.org.

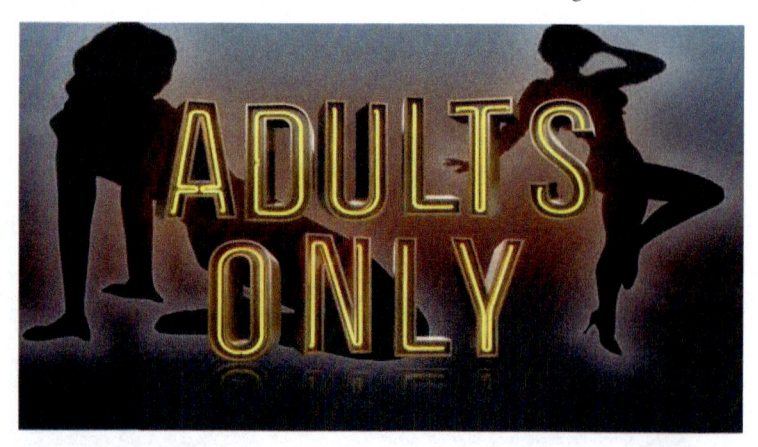

Burlesque Hall of Fame
Located in the Arts District, this is the only museum in the world dedicated to the history of burlesque (entertainment that includes dancing, sketches, chorus numbers, and striptease). You'll tour a collection of costumes, memorabilia, props, and ephemera from the heyday of burlesque to today.

The museum showcases several thousand costumes, stage props, photographs, and personal effects documenting the careers and lives of burlesque performers. *Info*: 1027 S. Main St., Suite #110. Tel. 888/661-6465. The museum offers guided tours hourly on Tue, Wed, Fri, and Sat from 11am to 5pm (last entry at 4pm), and on Sun from noon to 5pm (last entry at 4pm). Admission: $18. burlesquehall.com.

Sportsbook at Circa Resort
This resort and casino opened in 2020. It's downtown on the Fremont Street Experience (*see page 37*) and is the first new building constructed in the area since 1980. Las Vegas Club, Mermaids Casino, and the Glitter Gulch strip club were all demolished to make way for the 35-story tower. The lobby showcases the former Vegas Vickie cowgirl neon sign, which was previously used at the strip club. Across the street is a nine-story parking garage known as Garage-Mahal. There's a two-story casino and a sportsbook. The three-story sportsbook is where you can wager on sports competitions, including football (the Super Bowl is the largest game for betting), baseball, basketball, hockey, soccer, horse racing, greyhound racing, and fighting events. Stadium Swim has six pools over three levels, private cabanas, day beds, chaise lounge chairs, swim-up bars, and a gigantic 40-foot tall screen broadcasting sporting events. *Info*: 8 Fremont St. Tel. 702/247-2258. www.circalasvegas.com.

Downtown Sights

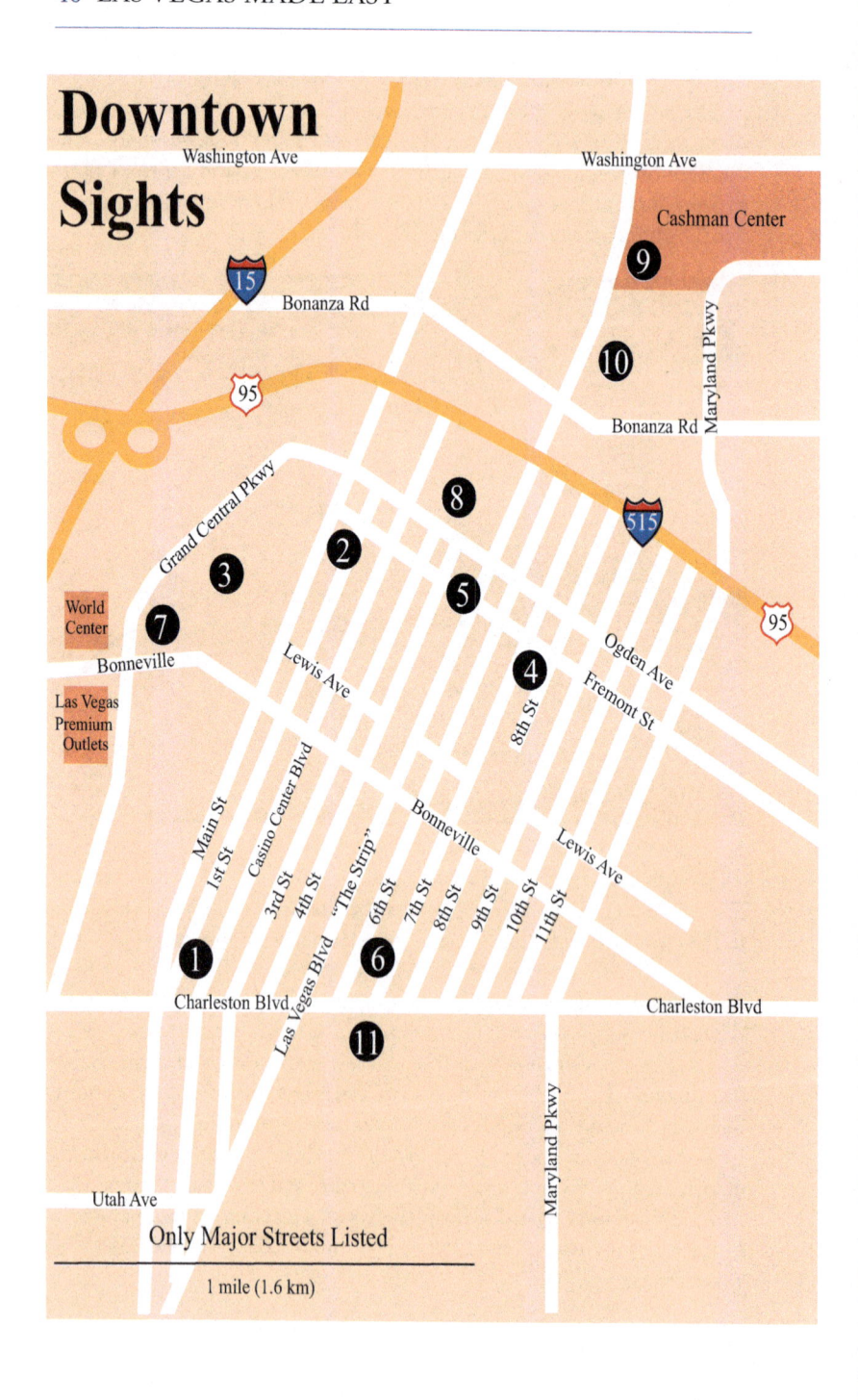

Downtown Sights Map
1. Arts District (18b)/ Burlesque Museum
2. Circa Resort & Casino
3. Discovery Children's Museum
4. Downtown Container Park
5. Fremont Street Experience
6. Gold & Silver Pawn Shop
7. Melting Building (Lou Ruvo Center for Brain Health)
8. Mob Museum
9. Natural History Museum
10. Neon Museum
11. Zak Bagans' Haunted Museum

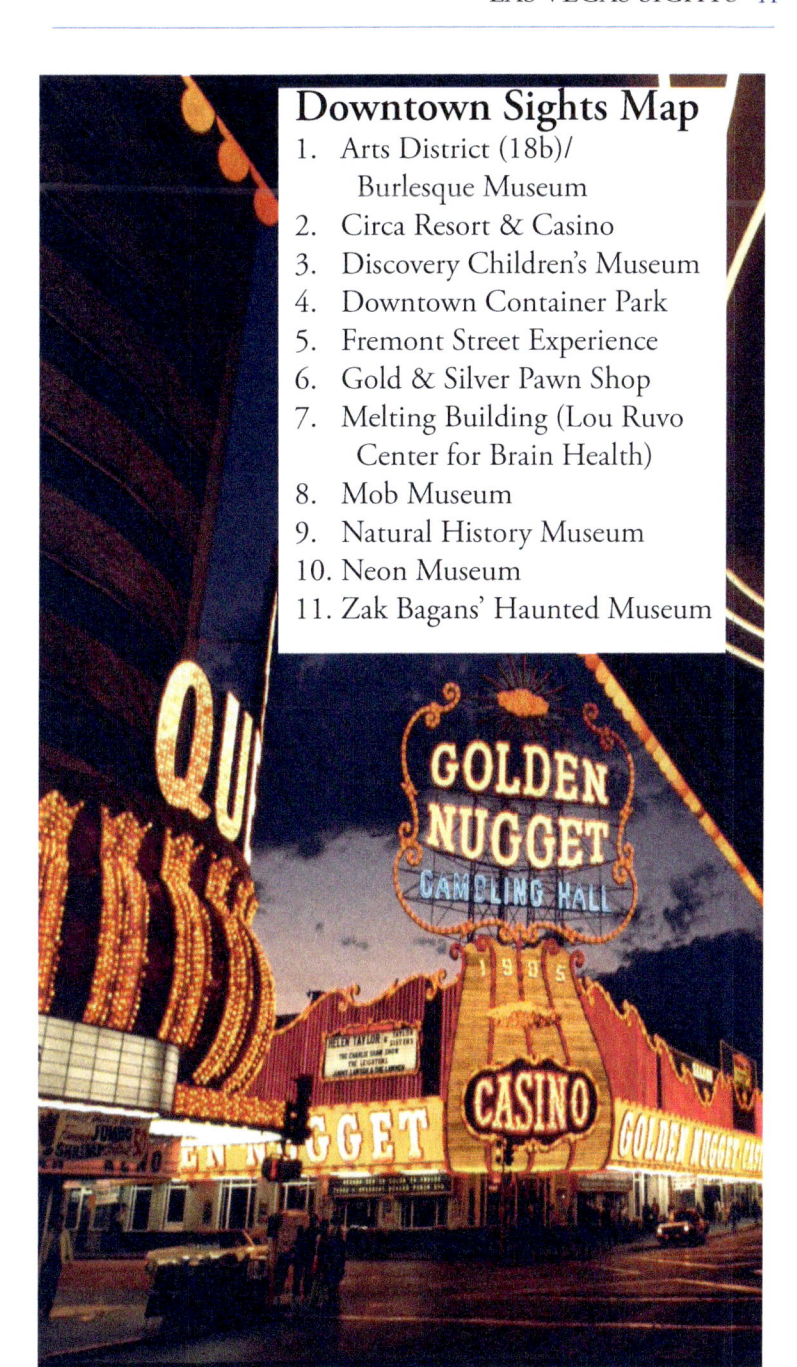

Mob Museum

The Mob Museum tells the story of how the mafia operated in Las Vegas and of the prosecution of mobsters. It's in the former federal courthouse where, in 1950, the Kefauver Committee held hearings on organized crime. The electric chair that was used on gangsters, and spies Ethel and Julius Rosenberg, has been reconstructed. One exhibit highlights the 1929 Valentine's Day Massacre, where seven members of a bootlegging gang were lined up against a wall in a garage in Chicago and shot. Part of the wall has been rebuilt in the museum. You can also visit The Underground in the basement. This distillery and "speakeasy" features artifacts from the 1920s and Prohibition-era craft cocktails. *Info:* 300 Stewart Ave. Tel. 702/229-2734. Museum open daily 9am-9pm. Speakeasy open Mon-Wed 11am-10pm, Thu and Fri 11am-midnight, Sun noon-midnight. Admission: From $29.95. Parking is available in the lot next to the museum for $8 for four hours. www.themobmuseum.org.

Gold and Silver Pawn Shop

You'll know this famous pawn shop from the History Channel's show *Pawn Stars*. This reality television series featured the shop and the haggling with its owner over prices. You'll find lots of interesting stuff to buy or look at, including Super Bowl rings, Rolex watches, jewelry, coins, comic books, and firearms. You might even catch a glimpse of the show's stars: Rick, Corey, Chumlee, and "The Old Man." *Info:* 713 S. Las Vegas Blvd. Tel. 702/385-7912. Open daily 10am-5:30pm (Thu-Sat until 7pm). Admission: Free. Parking is free. gspawn.com.

Discovery Children's Museum

Las Vegas isn't just for adult visitors. This three-story museum is in Symphony Park, adjacent to the Smith Center for Performing Arts. The museum features exhibits on science, technology, engineering, and math and is aimed at toddlers to pre-teens. *The Summit* is a 12-story tower of play space and interactive activities. Other exhibits include *Toddler Town*, *Eco City*, and *Young at Art*. Exhibits change frequently. *Info:* 360 Promenade Place. Tel. 702/382-3445. Open Tue-Sat 10am-5pm, Sun noon-5pm. Open Mon during school breaks. Admission: $16. www.discoverykidslv.org

"Melting Building"
The Cleveland Clinic Lou Ruvo Center for Brain Health looks like it is melting in the Nevada sun. World-renowned architect Frank Gehry designed the building in 2010. It's only open for patient care and evening events. The interesting building is near the Discovery Children's Museum. *Info*: 888 W. Bonneville Ave.

Las Vegas Natural History Museum
Another option for kids is Nevada's interactive natural history museum. Galleries include *Treasures of Egypt*, *Marine Life* (with sharks and stingrays), *African Safari*, *Wild Nevada*, *Dinosaur Mummy*, *Prehistoric Life*, and *International Wildlife*. *Info*: 900 N. Las Vegas Blvd. Tel. 702/384-3466. Open daily 9am-4pm. Admission: $14, ages 12-18 $12. www.lvnhm.org.

Zak Bagans' Haunted Museum
Interested in the paranormal? This 30-room property, in downtown Las Vegas, was built in 1938. Throughout the years, there have been rumors of ghosts roaming the house. Dark rituals took place in the basement during the 1970s. The property appeared in the Travel Channel series *Ghost Adventures*. You can wander through its halls and secret passages. The museum's collection includes possessions of notorious serial killers. Some exhibits include Charles Manson's ashes, Dr. Jack Kevorkian's death van (where he assisted terminally ill patients to end their lives), and the "Propofol Chair" from Michael Jackson's death room. Also here is "Peggy the Doll," said to have caused nosebleeds, fainting, and a heart attack when looking into her eyes. Creepy! *Info*: 600 E. Charleston Blvd. Tel. 702/444-0744. Open Wed-Mon 10am-8pm. Closed Tue. Admission: From $48 (two-hour tour). Must be age 14 and over. Late nights flashlight tours and psychic readings at additional cost. thehauntedmuseum.com.

Downtown Container Park
The Downtown Container Park, on Fremont Street, is a unique shopping, dining, and entertainment complex made entirely from shipping containers. The park is fronted by a massive metal mantis and features stacked containers. In the containers, you will find shops selling handmade jewelry, local art, clothing, and eateries. The park also has a large playground, making it a family-friendly destination. Kids and adults can climb the three-story treehouse which features an adventurous slide. Events such as live music performances, yoga classes, and movie nights create a vibrant atmosphere for locals and tourists. The park is for adults only after 9pm. Some of the interesting activities here include an indoor golf area, virtual reality experiences, arcade, flight simulator, zip lines, and even an ax-throwing station. Hungry? Head to The Beast, a food hall found in the belly of a dragon, or relax and dine at Downtown Terrace. For cocktails, try Oak & Ivy. *Info*: 707 Fremont St. Tel. 702/359-9982. Open Mon-Thu 11:30am-8pm. Fri and Sat 11am-9pm, Sun 11am-8pm. www.downtowncontainerpark.com.

WEDDING CHAPELS

Las Vegas has long been known as a destination for speedy and inexpensive weddings. Nevada does not have a waiting period attached to their wedding licenses, so it's easy to get married with little advanced planning. There are over 50 wedding chapels in the city. Here are some of the most well-known and popular places to get hitched!

A Little White Wedding Chapel

Opened in 1951, this chapel has a long list of celebrity weddings, including Judy Garland, Frank Sinatra, Joan Collins, Michael Jordan, Demi Moore, and Britney Spears. If you're in a hurry, just drive your car through the "Drive Through Tunnel of Vows." *Info*: 1301 S. Las Vegas Blvd. Tel. 702/382-5943. Open daily 9am-9pm. From $80. www.alittlewhitechapel.com.

Chapel of the Flowers

Weddings, vow renewals, and commitment ceremonies have been taking place at this chapel on The Strip for over 60 years. There are quite a few packages to choose from, and you also can hold a reception here. The basic wedding starts at $299, but there are many choices for additional services like flowers and photos. *Info*: 1717 S. Las Vegas Blvd. Tel. 702/735-4331. Open daily. From $299. www.littlechapel.com.

Graceland Wedding Chapel

The oldest wedding chapel in Las Vegas opened in 1939. Elvis-theme weddings have been popular here since "The King" died. It claims to be the first chapel to hold an Elvis-theme wedding in Las Vegas. There's a notable list of celebrities that have been married here, including Billy Ray Cyrus, Aaron Neville, and Jon Bon Jovi. *Info*: 619 S. Las Vegas Blvd. Tel. 702/382-0091. Open daily 9am-11pm. Elvis Weddings From $249. www.gracelandchapel.com.

Elvis Chapel

This mid-century modern venue is another chapel with an Elvis theme. The officiant is an Elvis impersonator who serenades you during the ceremony. You can even have Elvis walk you down the aisle as part of the "Elvis Memories Package." *Info*: 1320 S. Casino Center Blvd. Tel. 702/383-5909. Open daily 9am-9pm. From $295. elvischapel.com.

The Little Neon Chapel

This chapel in the heart of downtown on Fremont Street Experience features affordable weddings. They even have mobster-theme weddings, so you can get married by your favorite most wanted criminal. *Info*: 450 Fremont St. Tel. 702/418-2994. Open daily 10am-8:30pm (Sat until 10pm). From $69. www.thelittleneonchapel.com.

FURTHER AFIELD

While there is plenty to do on The Strip and downtown, Las Vegas offers more if you're willing to leave the slot machines and neon lights behind for a while. You can visit the birthplace of Las Vegas at Springs Preserve, drive a Maserati at SpeedVegas, or feed a giraffe and view majestic lions up close at Lion Habitat Ranch. There's so much to do in Greater Las Vegas. In another chapter of this book, we'll head outside of the city for day trips and excursions.

Springs Preserve
The Springs Preserve celebrates the birthplace of Las Vegas. The Las Vegas Springs, the original water source for Las Vegas, form the centerpiece of the preserve. This 180-acre site showcases the history of Las Vegas and provides a vision for a sustainable future in the desert. Springs Preserve has botanical gardens, galleries, concerts, and frequent events. The walking trails that wind through a wetland habitat are a highlight.

Also here is the **Nevada State Museum** (admission included with entry to the preserve). You'll see Nevada's state fossil (an Ichthyosaur Shonisaurus popularis), step inside a stalactite cave, view an atomic explosion, watch holographic figures tell the story of the state's miners, and learn the history of Las Vegas.

It's approximately three miles (4.8 km) west of downtown Las Vegas. A welcome change from the glitz and noise of The Strip. *Info*: 333 S. Valley View Blvd. Tel. 702/822-7700. Open Thu-Mon 9am-4pm. Admission: $18.95, $10.95 ages 3-17 (discounts for Nevada residents). www.springsreserve.org.

SpeedVegas
Have you ever wanted to drive a Lamborghini, Maserati, or Porsche? Then head to the SpeedVegas Supercar Driving Experience. You can take a spin for five laps from $249. Want a vehicle for a day? You can drive a McLaren for $2,490. Vegas Superkarts has a go-kart racetrack (from $35) or you can have an off-road experience in a Baja Race Truck (from $299 for five laps). If you have a need for speed, this is the place! *Info*: 14200 S. Las Vegas Blvd. Tel. 702/213-9068. Open daily 9am-5pm. www.speedvegas.com.

Las Vegas Motor Speedway
This complex has a 1.5 mile (2.4 km) tri-oval and infield and outfield road courses. It includes a paved short track oval, drag strip, and dirt courses. The speedway hosts NASCAR races and NHRA drag events. There's a full calendar of evening and night races at the track's Bullring. It's also a popular venue for music concerts. The speedway is located 15 miles (24 km) northeast of The Strip. *Info*: 7000 N. Las Vegas Blvd. Tel. 800/644-4444. www.lvms.com.

Las Vegas Grand Prix
The Las Vegas Grand Prix is part of the Formula One World Championship. The night race is a 3.8 mile (6.1 km) course that passes some of the city's landmarks, casinos, and hotels. Speeds on the course reach up to 212 mph (341 kph). The inaugural race was held in November 2023. Formula One has signed a ten-year agreement to hold the event in Las Vegas. *Info*: www.f1lasvegasgp.com.

LAS VEGAS SIGHTS 49

Lion Habitat Ranch
Located in Henderson, not too far from The Strip, is this habitat with 40 kings of the jungle. Not only are there lions, but parrots, tortoises, ostriches, and a giraffe. Most of the animals and birds at this non-profit organization are pet surrenders and rescues. You can feed the giraffe ($10), feed a lion ($100), or have the giraffe create some artwork for you ($100). The habitat is a fine way to get up close to these majestic animals. *Info*: 382 Bruner Ave. in Henderson. Tel. 702/595-6666. Open Thu-Mon 11am-3pm. Closed Tue and Wed. Admission: $25 includes one child ages 4-14, $10 each additional child. www.lionhabitatranch.org.

Seven Magic Mountains
Seven 11-story-tall rock towers sit forlornly in the desert 20 miles (32 km) south of The Strip. In 2016, Swiss artist Ugo Rondinone collected gigantic Nevada boulders, painted them in bright fluorescent colors, and then had them stacked to create his work of art. It's not for everyone, but people visit the desert at all times of the day to take a photo with the art installation. *Info*: From Las Vegas, take Interstate 15 South to Sloan Road (exit 25). Turn left (east) to Las Vegas Boulevard. Drive approximately seven miles (11.2 km) south on Las Vegas Boulevard. The art installation is on your left. Note that you can see the boulders from Interstate 15. Admission and parking are free. Use your cell phone to learn about the art and the artist by calling 702/381-5182. sevenmagicmountains.com.

Dig This

This "amusement park" lets you take out your frustrations and brings out the inner construction worker in you. You can operate bulldozers and drive excavators at this spot in the desert. Feel like crushing a car? Then, you've come to the right place. Adults can drive a skid steer track loader for $175 an hour. Kids can dig on a one-ton, child-safe mini excavator on a mini-construction site. The park is located 12 miles (19.3 km) south of The Strip. Kids ages two to five and under 48" (1.22 meters) can operate with the assistance of a parent or guardian (no additional cost for a parent or guardian). Kids over 48" can operate independently. Kid prices from $25. Quite the unique experience. *Info*: 800 W Roban Ave. Tel. 702/222-4344. Open daily 8am-4pm. Admission: From $175. www.digthisvegas.com.

Aviation Museum

You might visit this exhibit if you're stuck in the airport on a flight delay or have some time before your flight departs. Howard W. Cannon Aviation Museum is located in Harry Reid International Airport. Visitors can explore the history of aviation in Nevada from the first flight in 1920 through the introduction of jets. The museum's prime exhibit is above baggage claim, with additional exhibits throughout Terminal 1. Some items on display include pilot uniforms, airplane parts, vintage aviation photos, and a small private airplane hanging from the ceiling. *Info*: Terminal 1 of the Harry Reid International Airport, 5757 Wayne Newton Blvd. Tel. 702/455-7968. Open during airport hours. Admission: Free.

Ethel M Botanical Cactus Garden
Ethel was the matriarch of the company that made Mars chocolates and M&M's. Ethel M Chocolates sells chocolates from its factory in Henderson, outside of Las Vegas. You can tour the confection factory, but most come here to stroll the three-acre botanical garden. The garden is the largest in Nevada, with over 300 species of succulents and cacti. You'll find native desert plants and cacti from South America and Australia. This is also a sanctuary for birds. The garden is especially popular during the holidays when the cacti are adorned with sparkling lights. A bonus is that the garden is free. Henderson is 15 miles (24 km) southeast of The Strip. *Info*: 2 Cactus Garden Dr. in Henderson. Tel. 800/438-4356. Open daily 10am-10pm. Admission: Free. Self-guided chocolate factory tours are Mon-Fri 10am-3:30pm. Admission: Free.
www.ethelm.com/pages/botanical-cactus-garden.

Shelby Heritage Center

Carroll Hall Shelby is sometimes referred to as the father of the "muscle car." He was an automotive designer and race car driver, best known for his involvement with the AC Cobra and Mustang for Ford Motor Company. He established Shelby American in 1962 to manufacture performance vehicles. If you're a "gear head," you won't want to miss visiting this home to over 25 Shelby vehicles. Among the vehicles on display is the first Cobra roadster CSX2000 that Shelby built. A guided tour takes 90 minutes, but you can wander around on your own for free. The center is part of the Shelby manufacturing facility. *Info*: 6405 Ensworth St. (at Sunset Rd. and across from Town Square). Tel. 702/942-7325. Open Mon-Sat 9:30am-5pm, Sun 10am-4pm. Admission: Free for self-guided tours. Guided tours from $49. www.shelby.com.

Nostalgia Street Rods

There is no shortage in and around Las Vegas of museums dedicated to the American love of vehicles. This museum includes a multi-million dollar collection of race cars, street rods, and scooters. There's also a selection of sports memorabilia with items from Mohammad Ali, Kobe Bryant, Arnold Palmer, and other notables in the history of sport. The music collection includes signed items from famous performers such as Elvis Presley and Jimi Hendrix. *Info*: 5375 Cameron St. in Henderson. 3.5 miles (5.6 km) from The Strip. Tel 702/876-3652. Open Mon-Fri 9am-4pm. Admission: $21.65. nostalgiastreetrods.com.

SPORTS TEAMS

Las Vegas isn't just a destination for gambling and entertainment. It's now popular for sports fans to visit the city to view professional sports in some of the best venues in the U.S.

National Football League (NFL)
Las Vegas Raiders
Allegiant Stadium, 3333 Al Davis Way
www.raiders.com

Women's National Basketball Association (WNBA)
Las Vegas Aces
Michelob ULTRA Arena (in Mandalay Bay Resort & Casino),
3950 S. Las Vegas Blvd.
aces.wnba.com

National Hockey League (NHL)
Vegas Golden Knights
T-Mobile Arena, 3780 S. Las Vegas Blvd.
www.nhl.com/goldenknights/

USL Championship (Men's Soccer League)
Las Vegas Lights FC
Cashman Field, 850 N. Las Vegas Blvd.
www.lasvegaslightsfc.com

Minor League Baseball (MiLB)
Las Vegas Aviators
(Triple-A affiliate of the Oakland Athletics)
Las Vegas Ballpark, 1650 S. Pavilion Center Dr.
www.milb.com/las-vegas

American Hockey League (AHL)
Henderson Silver Knights
(affiliate of the Vegas Golden Knights)
The Dollar Loan Center, 200 S. Green Valley Pkwy., Henderson
www.hendersonsilverknights.com

National Association for Stock Car Auto Racing (NASCAR)
Las Vegas Motor Speedway, 7000 N. Las Vegas Blvd.
www.lvms.com

Major League Baseball has approved the relocation of the Oakland Athletics baseball team to Las Vegas. A stadium will be built where the Tropicana Hotel is located. The Tropicana will close in April 2024.

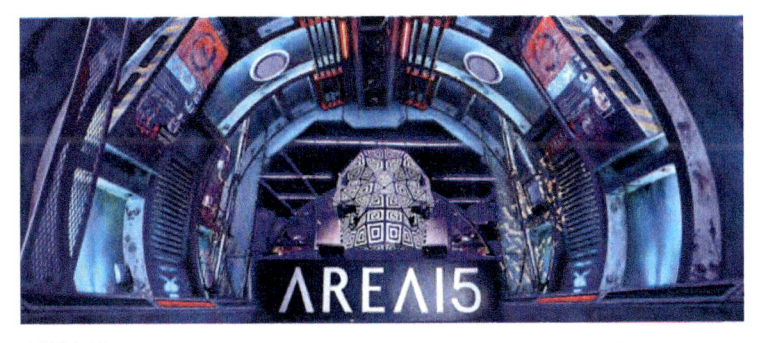

AREA15
Area15 is hard to describe, and perhaps that's what makes it so interesting. A short distance from The Strip, it's an immersive entertainment complex with a quirky blend of art and technology. If you're looking for something different from the stereotypical Las Vegas experience, come here. Relieve some stress while axe-throwing, try the flight simulator or zip line, have a virtual reality experience, take in a concert at the outdoor event space, and explore huge artwork from Art Island at the Burning Man festival. The Omega Mart is a supermarket where, through a beverage cooler, you enter a mysterious fun house. Entry is free, but you should reserve an entry pass online. In the evening, Area15 turns into a space for those over 18. There are lots of eating and drinking venues, including a hidden bar. Truly a unique destination. *Info*: S. Rancho Dr. (at Desert Inn and Interstate 15). Open daily 11am-11pm (Fri and Sat until 1am). You must be 18 and over after 9pm on Fri and Sat (with identification). Admission: Free. Certain "experiences" have entry fees. area15.com.

Las Vegas Farm
If you're looking for a family-friendly activity on weekends, head to the Las Vegas Farm. The farm offers visitors an opportunity to get up close with peacocks, ducks, geese, cows, pigs, llamas, rabbits (at the "Rabbitat"), tortoises, and more. A unique feature is the ability to feed some animals. You can purchase a bag of hay ($2) and the staff will instruct you on how to feed the animals. Kids and adults love it! There's a market and the Barn Buddies Sanctuary, housing rescued abused, neglected, and abandoned animals. *Info*: 7222 W. Grand Teton Dr. Tel. 702/982-8000. Open Sat and Sun from 9am-4pm. Admission: $10, $5 ages 12 and under. www.thelasvegasfarm.com. At the neighboring Gilcrease Orchard, you can hand pick fresh seasonal produce from the tree. The orchard is open in the fall and for special events. Check their website for events. *Info*: 7800 N. Tenaya. Tel. 702/409-0655. Admission: From $5. thegilcreaseorchard.org.

LAS VEGAS FOR KIDS

Las Vegas has aggressively marketed itself as a family-friendly destination. Here are a few of the activities featured in this book for children and young adults.

- **High Roller**

Soar above Las Vegas, on the largest observation wheel in North America. *See page 21.*

- **Adventuredome**

Have fun at an indoor amusement park with rides and attractions, including the Canyon Blaster roller coaster. *See page 24.*

- **Shark Reef Aquarium**

Get up close to sharks, giant rays, and exotic fish. *See page 25.*

- **Big Apple Coaster**

Reach speeds of up to 67 miles (108 km) per hour on this roller coaster! There's also a large game arcade. *See page 26.*

- **Madame Tussauds Wax Museum**

Take a selfie with your favorite star. *See page 26.*

- **Escape Game Las Vegas**

Escape from multiple rooms and choose themes and difficulties. *See page 27.*

- **Pinball Hall of Fame**

Play on over 1,000 classic pinball and video games. *See page 28.*

- **The Mirage Volcano**

Watch a volcano that explodes into flames, with eruptions of water, and a choreographed soundtrack. *See page 31.*

- **SlotZilla**

Ride a slot machine-inspired zip line that takes you above the Fremont Street Experience. *See page 37.*

- **Discovery Children's Museum**

Toddlers to pre-teens can probe exhibits on science, technology, engineering, and math. *See page 42.*

- **Las Vegas Natural History Museum**

Explore Nevada's interactive natural history museum. *See page 43.*

- **Nevada State Museum at Springs Preserve**

Learn the history of Las Vegas at this kid-friendly museum. *See page 47.*

- **Las Vegas Farm**

Feed the animals at this family-friendly weekend spot. *See page 55.*

A HISTORY OF GAMBLING IN LAS VEGAS

You can gamble at the airport, grocery store, gas station, and, of course, one of the 60 major casinos. How did the city become the gambling capital of the United States? Here's a brief history of gambling in "Sin City."

• Paiute tribes settled in what we now call Nevada as far back as 1100.

• In the 1800s, the area that is now Las Vegas was a stop along the trade route from east to west. The city's name is from the Spanish word "vegas" meaning "meadows."

• Developers build a railroad stop between Los Angeles and Salt Lake City in 1905.

• Gambling is banned in Nevada in 1909. Although gambling was illegal, some underground casinos flourished.

• In 1931, gambling is legalized and The Pair-O-Dice Club opens and becomes the city's first casino.

• Construction on the nearby Hoover Dam in the 1930s brings workers flocking to the city.

• The Prohibition Act is repealed in 1933.

• The first hotel resort, El Rancho Vegas, opens in 1941.

• In 1946, gangster Bugsy Siegel opens the large Flamingo Hotel and Casino. Other resorts follow.

• During the 1960s, The Rat Pack, Howard Hughes, and other celebrities help Las Vegas grow as an entertainment destination.

• In the 1980s and 1990s, Las Vegas sees the rise of mega resorts, like MGM, Treasure Island, and the Bellagio.

• The 2000s see the continued growth and popularity of Las Vegas as a gambling, entertainment, and vacation destination.

THE LGBTQ+ SCENE
Las Vegas is a big destination for LGBTQ+ visitors. There are many venues that cater to gay visitors and many of them are open 24 hours. Gay life here is vibrant and varied. Here are some of the gay establishments you'll find in the city.

- **Badlands.** Country theme bar with pool tables, darts, and shows. 953 Sahara Ave #22B. Tel. 702/792-9262. Open 24 hours. badlandsbarlv.com.
- **The Garden.** Cocktails, live events, and food in a chic garden-type bar in the arts district. 1017 S 1st St #180. Tel. 702/202-0900. Thu and Fri 6pm-2am, Sat 11am-2am, Sun 11am-5pm (drag brunch/reservations needed). thegardenslasvegas.com.
- **The Garage.** Bar with a garage theme offering pool, darts, gaming, and food. 1487 E Flamingo Rd. C. Tel. 702/440-6333. Open 24 hours. thegaragelv.com.
- **Phoenix Bar and Lounge.** Laid back bar with a lounge feel, karaoke, pool, and a dance floor. 4213 Sahara Ave Tel. 702/826-2422. Open 24 hours. thephoenixlv.com.
- **Queen Bar.** Cocktails, live music, dancing, and drag at this fun club. 1215 S. Las Vegas Blvd. Tel. 702/982-8259. Thu 6pm-2am, Fri 6pm-4am, Sat 6pm-5am, Sun noon-2am. queenlv.com.
- **The Back Door.** Nightspot with dance floor, Latin music, and drag performances. 1415 Charleston Blvd. Tel. 702/831-0621. Open Fri-Sun 10:30pm-6am. www.facebook.com//thebackdoor/.
- **Quadz.** Video bar with gaming, pool, and darts. 4640 Paradise Rd. Tel. 702/733-0383. Open 24 hours. quadz.bar.

LAS VEGAS SIGHTS 59

- **Piranha Nightclub.** Lush nightclub with theme nights, drag, VIP area, bottle service, and patio. 4633 Paradise Rd. Tel. 702/791-0100. Open Sun-Thu 10pm-5am, Fri and Sat 10pm-6am. paranhavegas.com.
- **Fun Hog Ranch.** Daily drink specials, jukebox, and video poker in a relaxed environment (cash only). 495 E. Twain Ave. Tel. 702/791-7001. Open 24 hours. funhogranchlv.com.
- **Free Zone.** Club with karaoke, drag, gaming, food, pool, and dancing. 610 E. Naples Dr. Tel. 702/794-2300. Open 24 hours. freezonelv.com.
- **Flex Cocktail Lounge.** Bar, club, and lounge with a small-town feel. 501 E. Twain Ave. Tel. 702/385-3839. Open 24 hours. flexlasvegas.com.
- **Las Vegas Eagle.** Leather bar in a strip mall with special events. 3430 Tropicana Ave., Suite 47. Tel 702/458-8662. Open 24 hours. facebook.com/thelasvegaseagle/.
- **Gipsy.** Iconic nightclub. 4605 Paradise Rd. Tel. 702/731-1919. Open Thu 10pm-4am, Fri 7pm-4am, Sat 10pm-4am, Sun 10pm-3am. gipsylasvegas.com.
- **Hamburger Mary's.** American bar and grill with quirky entertainment. 1700 E. Flamingo Rd. Tel. 702/592-0208. Open Fri 7pm-10pm, Sat and Sun 11am-2am. hamburgermarys.com.
- **Don't Tell Mama.** Cozy lounge featuring singing servers and piano accompaniment for open mike opportunities. 450 Freemont St., Suite 167. Tel 702/207-0788. Open Tue-Thu 8pm-2:30am, Fri and Sat 8pm-3:30am, Sun 8pm-2am. donttellmama.com.
- **The Valley Saloon.** Establishment featured on the television show *Bar Rescue*. 3328 Charleston Blvd. Tel 702/457-3353. Open 24 hours.
- **Raised by Wolves.** Trendy bar with great cocktails and live performances. 450 Fremont St., Suite 251 (upstairs). Open Wed-Sun 5pm-4am. Tel. 702/832-5564. raisedbywolveslv.com.
- **Hard Hat Lounge.** Dive bar with pub grub. 1675 Industrial Rd. Tel 702/384-8987. Open 24 hours. hardhatlounglv.com.

Drag Brunches
- **The Garden.** 1017 S 1st St #180. Tel. 702/202-0900. Sat and Sun. thegardenlasvegas.com (reservations required).
- **Hamburger Mary's.** 1700 E. Flamingo Rd. Tel. 702/592-0208. Sat and Sun at noon. hamburgermarys.com.
- **Señor Frogs.** In Treasure Island Hotel & Casino. 3300 S. Las Vegas Blvd. Tel. 702/912-9525. Fri-Sun. senorfrogs.com.
- **Drag Brunch Las Vegas.** 3300 S. Las Vegas Blvd. Tel. 888/885-8677. Fri-Sun. vossevents.com.

- **Diva Royale Drag Queens.** 450 Fremont St. Tel. 702/960-0685. Thu-Sun dinner shows, Sat 1:30pm brunch, Sun 3:30pm brunch. dragqueensshow.com.
- **Illusions the Drag Queen Show.** 174 S. Las Vegas Blvd. Tel. 833/783-3648. Brunch and dinner shows. illusionsthedragqueenshow.com.

Saunas/Sex Clubs
- **Entourage Vegas Spa and Health Club.** Gay spa with pool, stream room, sauna, and social areas. 953 E. Sahara Ave. A19. Tel. 702/650-9191. Open 24 hours. vegasgayspa.com.
- **Kuma Club.** Private health and social club with sauna, showers, and intimate spaces. 700 E. Naples Dr. #107. Tel. 725/225-8800. Open Sun-Thu 4pm-4am, Fri and Sat 4pm-6am. kumaclublv.com.

Retail
- **Get Booked.** Retailer carrying a selection of gay pride goods. 4640 Paradise Rd. Tel. 702/737-7780. Open daily 11am-7pm. getbooked.com.

Pool Party
- **Luxor.** Huge casino and resort with "Temptation Sundays" LGBTQ+ pool party. 3900 S. Las Vegas Blvd. Tel. 877/386-4658, Sun May-Sep. luxor.mgmresorts.com/en/nightlife/temptation-sundays.html.

Sleeping
- **Bent Inn & Pub.** LGBTQ+ boutique hotel downtown (adults only). 1100 Ogden Ave. Tel. 725/305-9458. Open 24 hours. bentinn.com.

SHOPPING

Las Vegas is known for an array of shopping options. Here are some of the most popular shopping areas.

The Forum Shops at Caesars

Shopping mall, connected to the Caesars Palace Resort, with over 160 stores and restaurants. You'll find everything from Armani to Levi's. *Info*: The Strip and Flamingo Road. www.simon.com/mall/the-forum-shops-at-caesars-palace.

Town Square

This outdoor shopping, entertainment, and dining complex, on the south end of The Strip, has a mix of chain stores, boutique shops, eateries, and movie theaters. *Info*: 6605 S. Las Vegas Blvd. www.mytownsquarelasvegas.com.

LINQ Promenade

The LINQ is an open-air retail, entertainment, and dining district on The Strip. There are over 35 stores here and is a popular dining destination with eateries such as Brooklyn Bowl, Gordon Ramsay Fish and Chips, and In-N-Out Burger. After you've bought your gifts and filled your belly, you can take a ride on the observation wheel, the High Roller. *Info*: 3535 S. Las Vegas Blvd. www.caesars.com/linq/things-to-do/shopping.

Grand Canal Shoppes

This large shopping center is at The Venetian Hotel and Resort on The Strip. It's a recreation of the streets of Venice, Italy. Browse the upscale shops along the cobblestone lanes. After you're done shopping, take a break at one of the many restaurants or even take a gondola ride along the canal. *Info*: 3377 S. Las Vegas Blvd. www.grandcanalshoppes.com.

Via Bellagio

At the Bellagio Resort, you can stroll along Via Bellagio, a "street" that's home to such luxurious boutiques as Gucci, Chanel, and Armani. *Info*: 3600 S. Las Vegas Blvd. www.bellagio.com.

Fashion Show Mall
One of the largest shopping centers in Las Vegas, with over 250 stores, is conveniently located on The Strip. A unique feature is the live runway shows frequently held in the center of the mall. Some stores include Macy's, Dick's Sporting Goods, Dillard's, Neiman Marcus, Nordstrom, and Saks Fifth Avenue. *Info*: 3200 S. Las Vegas Blvd. www.fslv.com.

Miracle Mile Shops
There are over 150 stores at this shopping center at the Planet Hollywood Resort. You'll find apparel, art, fashion accessories, beauty products, souvenirs, and gifts. *Info*: 3667 S. Las Vegas Blvd. www.miraclemileshopslv.com.

The Shoppes at Mandalay Place
The Shoppes are on the sky bridge between the Mandalay Bay and Luxor resorts. Fun shops include Flip Flop Shop, Ron Jon Surf Shop, and Suite 160. It's a popular destination for dining, with options like Slice of Vegas, Ri Ra Irish Pub, and Minus5 Ice Lounge. *Info*: 3950 S. Las Vegas Blvd. mandalaybay.mgmresorts.com/en/amenities/the-shoppes-at-mandalay-bay-place.html.

Crystals at CityCenter
High-end shoppers can enjoy what is claimed to be the highest concentration of designer flagship stores in the world. Take your pick from Versace, Valentino, Dolce & Gabbana, or Tom Ford. *Info*: 3720 S. Las Vegas Blvd. www.simon.com/mall/the-shops-at-crystals.

Las Vegas North Premium Outlets
Bargain shopping is the main attraction of this outdoor mall in downtown Las Vegas. Some shops that have outlets here include Tommy Hilfiger, Adidas, DKNY, and Michael Kors. *Info*: 875 S. Grand Central Pkwy. www.premiumoutlets.com/outlet/las-vegas-north.

➤ Downtown Summerlin
Summerlin is a short drive west of The Strip. There's an outdoor shopping center with over 125 stores, restaurants, and movie theaters. A popular market is held on Saturdays from 9am-2pm. Also here are the Las Vegas Ballpark, home of the minor league Las Vegas Aviators, and City National Arena, the practice facility of the NHL Vegas Golden Knights. *Info*: 14 miles (22.5 km) via Interstate15 North. 1980 Festival Plaza Dr. summerlin.com/downtown-summerlin/.

POOL SCENE

Whether you're visiting friends, renting a home, or staying in a hotel, you'll likely have access to a pool where you can start your day with a refreshing dip, spend your day lounging, or relax after a day of sightseeing. Some hotels in the city allow non-guests to hang out at the pool, with the added benefit of poolside bars. Here are a few to check out. Day passes can also be booked through resortpass.com.

Red Rock Casino, Hotel, & Spa

Red Rock has the finest pool off The Strip. Its large circular pool has smaller pools connected to it. You'll have fabulous views of the red rocks in the distance. Three acres of pools, private rental cabanas, kid areas, a waterfall island, and poolside gambling all make relaxing here a memorable experience. If you're not staying at the complex, you can spend the day at the pool from $30. *Info*: 11011 W. Charleston Blvd. Driving distance from The Strip is 11 miles (17.7 km). Tel.702/797-7777. www.redrockresort.com/see-and-do/pool/.

Circa Resort & Casino

The Stadium Swim at the Circa Resort in downtown Las Vegas is a unique experience. There are three levels in the pool complex, and it features six pools. If that's not enough, there's a massive 40-foot-tall high-definition screen broadcasting sports events. Swim-up bars, private cabana rentals, an attentive staff, and sports betting all add to the experience. Day bed rentals from $25. *Info*: 8 Fremont St. Tel. 702/247-2258. www.circalasvegas.com.

Caesars Palace
You'll need to reserve a cabana or daybed to enter the pools at the Caesars Palace Resort. If you do, you'll have seven pools to dip in. The "Garden of the Gods" pool complex has swim-up gambling, places to eat, and plenty of drinks available. The pool has fountains, Roman statues, and adult-only areas. *Info*: 3570 S. Las Vegas Blvd. Tel. 731-7280. Reservations from $100. www.caesars.com/caesars-palace/things-to-do/garden-of-the-gods-pool-oasis.

Mandalay Bay Resort and Casino
The Mandalay Bay Beach complex covers a whopping 11 acres and the wave pool holds 1.6 million gallons of water. While the main pool is closed during winter months, the upscale Moorea Beach Club is open all year. You can ride tides in the wave pool, lounge in the lagoon, and flow with the Lazy River. For food, dine at the Beach Bar and Grill and the complex has three bars. You can also rent daybeds and gazebos. *Info*: 3950 S. Las Vegas Blvd. Tel. 877/305-3136. Admission to pool for non-guests from $25. mandalaybay.mgmresorts.com.

The Cosmopolitan
This luxurious resort on The Strip has three pools. The lively Boulevard Pool features upbeat music and a party atmosphere, the Marquee Dayclub (closed in winter) features DJs, bottle service, and craft cocktails, and the Chelsea Pool is for those looking for a more chill experience. Cosmopolitan pools are a popular choice for group cabana rentals. *Info*: 3708 S. Las Vegas Blvd. Tel. 702/698-7000. Admission to pool for non-guests from $20. www.cosmopolitanlasvegas.com.

GOLFING

Las Vegas is a huge destination for golfers. There are over 50 golf courses within an hour's drive from Las Vegas, and some right within town. We've listed a few top golf courses.

Bali Hai Golf Club

You're in the desert, but this course has lush landscapes and lovely water features. Hundreds of palm trees and views of the Las Vegas skyline add to the experience. *Info*: 5160 S. Las Vegas Blvd. Tel. 702/597-2400. Designers: Brian Curley and Lee E. Schmidt. Par 71. 7002 yards (back tees)/5535 yards (front tees). www.balihaigolfclub.com.

Rio Secco Golf Club

This phenomenal golf club overlooks Las Vegas and has an interesting separation of holes. Six holes are on a plateau overlooking the city, six in a desert wash, and another six on gorgeous canyons. *Info*: 2851 Grand Hills Dr. in Henderson. Tel. 702/777-2400. Designers: Rees Jones, Keith Evans, and Steve Weisser. Par 71. 7215 yards (back tees)/5226 yards (back tees). www.golfriosecco.com.

Southshore Golf Club
Ascending from the shore of Lake Las Vegas into the hills of the desert, this course has incredible views. With elevation changes of over 300 feet along the way, this venue is a favorite of many golfers visiting Las Vegas. *Info*: 100 Strada Di Circolo in Henderson. Tel 702/856-8400. Designer: Jack Nicklaus. Par 71. 6918 yards (back tees)/4844 yards (front tees). www.southshoreccllv.com.

Las Vegas National Golf Club
Founded in 1961 and less than 10 minutes from The Strip, this popular course with lush fairways has hosted several LPGA & PGA events. In 1996, Tiger Woods captured his first PGA Tour victory here. *Info*: 1911 E. Desert Inn Rd. Tel. 702/889-1000. Designer: Bert Stamps. Par 71. 6614 yards (back tees)/5091 yards (front tees). www.lasvegasnational.com.

TPC Las Vegas
If you visit the Red Rock National Park on the outskirts of Las Vegas, you'll experience some of the desert's best landscapes and scenery. TPC Las Vegas, which is huddled in the footsteps of the picturesque national park, is located 20 minutes northwest of the city. The back nine holes are especially scenic. *Info*: 9851 Canyon Run Dr. Tel. 702/256-2500. Designers: Bobby Weed, Raymond Floyd, Ed Ault, and Tom Clark. Par 71. 7016 yards (back tees)/4869 (front tees). www.tpc.com/lasvegas

Atomic Golf
This golf and entertainment destination is spread over nearly seven acres. It has four bars, 103 hitting bays, and a putting district. The "Astrocade" is a large sports viewing area. *Info*: 1850 S. Main St. Tel. 702/899-4633. atomicgolf.com.

3. Excursions

- Spring Mountains National Recreation Area/ Mount Charleston
- Red Rock Canyon
- Valley of Fire
- Death Valley
- Mojave National Preserve
- Primm
- Laughlin
- Hoover Dam and Lake Mead
- Grand Canyon (West Rim)
- Pahrump

169
Valley of Fire
15
176
95
93
157
167
Mt. Charleston
147
Las Vegas
159
Lake Mead
Red Rock
166
160
Hoover Dam
Boulder City
15
161
93
Primm
95
NEVADA
CALIFORNIA
163
68
Laughlin

Spring Mountains National Recreation Area/Mount Charleston
This national recreation area, also commonly known as Mount Charleston, is a spring fed oasis that rises out of the Mojave Desert. Each season offers something different. In the summer, you can escape the brutal heat of the desert and cool off. Winter is a snowy paradise, autumn bursts with changing colors, and wildflowers dot the area in spring. The Charleston Peak rises to nearly 12,000 feet (3,658 meters). The recreation area has places for camping, picnics, biking, horseback riding, and off-road driving. You might even catch a glimpse of the wild horses that roam here. There are 19 trails in the recreation area for all skill levels. They range from easy trails, like the .8 mile (1.3 km) Echo/Little Falls Trail, to the difficult North Loop to Summit (Charleston Peak) at 10.3 miles (16.6 km). If you don't have the time, or energy, to hike, you can take a scenic drive through the recreation area. Spring Mountains are home to 25 plant and animal species that are not found anywhere else. Spring Mountain Visitor Gateway has a visitor center, two amphitheaters, an educational building, monuments to the Paiute tribes, and the first national **Cold War Memorial**. The drive from Las Vegas to Mount Charleston is 40 miles (64 km). *Info*: To reach Mount Charleston from Las Vegas, take US Route 95 North to Nevada Route 157 West. 2525 Kyle Canyon Rd. Tel. 702/872-5486. www.gomtcharleston.com. *At the time of publication, the visitor center and some trails were closed because of damage from Tropical Storm Hilary in August 2023.*

Red Rock Canyon

Tired of all that glitz and gambling? Get some fresh air, and enjoy the incredible views, at Red Rock Canyon. Located west of The Strip, the Red Rock Canyon National Conservation Area encompasses over 195,000 acres in the Mojave Desert. There are many hiking trails and a 13-mile (21 km) scenic drive winding through the canyon. Red Rock is a popular destination for horseback riding. Note that timed entry reservations are required for the scenic drive from October through May. *Info*: 1000 Scenic Loop Dr. (Visitor Center). Tel. 702/515-5350. Visitor center open daily from 8am-4:30pm. Scenic Drive open Nov-Feb 6am-5pm, Mar and Oct 6am-7pm, Apr-Sep 6am-8pm. Admission: Car/Truck for one day $20. Motorcycle for one day $10. Bicyclist for one day $8. Pedestrian for one day $5. Annual Pass $50. Discounts for seniors and military. 19 miles (30 km) from downtown Las Vegas. Take NV-613 and US 95 N to CC 215S. www.redrockcanyonlv.org. *See map on the next page.*

EXCURSIONS 71

Red Rock Canyon

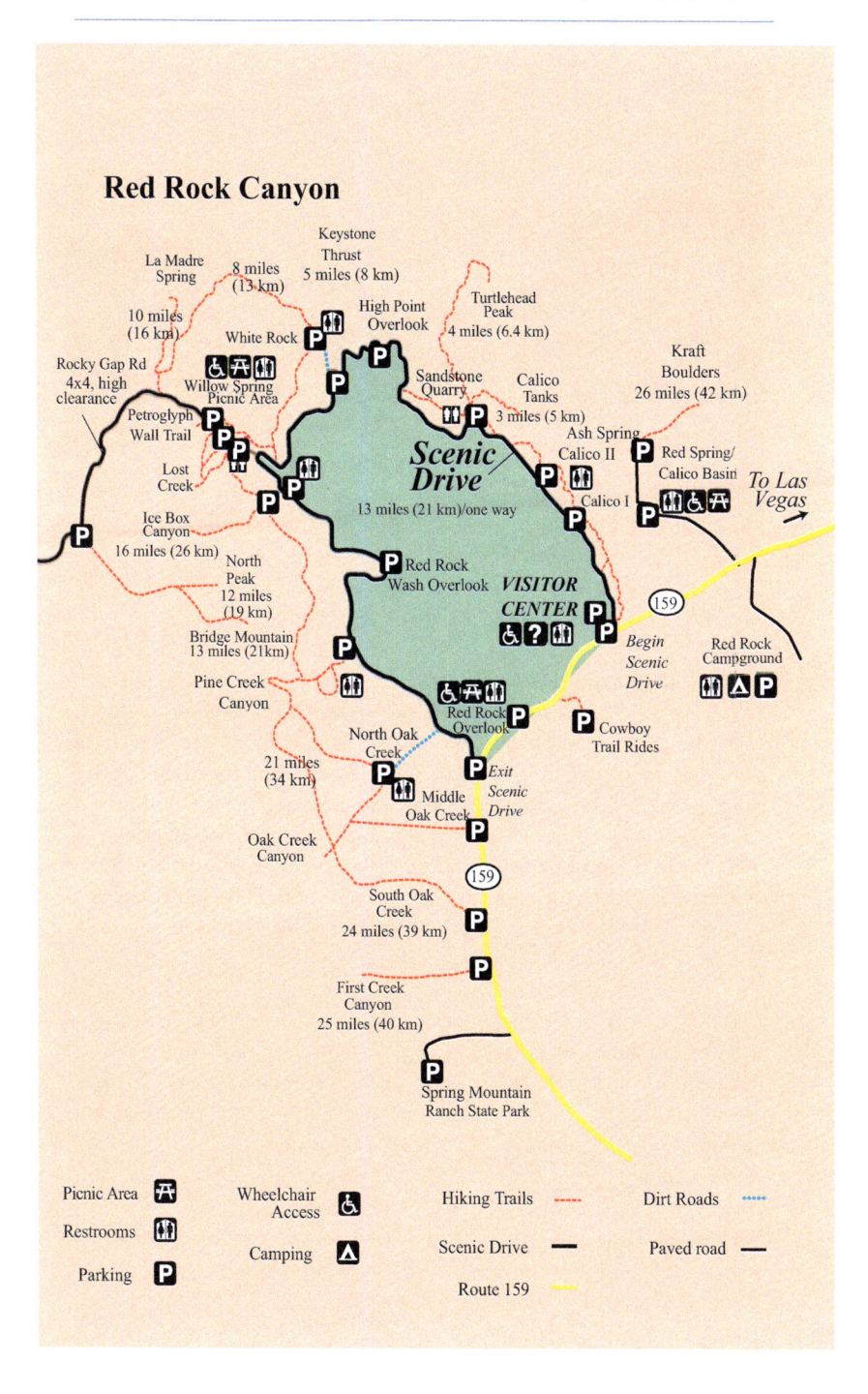

Valley of Fire State Park
From Las Vegas, take Interstate 15 North for about 33 miles. Take exit 75 and continue for 18 miles on the Valley of Fire Highway.

Nevada's largest and oldest state park is located 50 miles (80 km) northeast of Las Vegas. The park's over 40,000 acres contain brilliant Aztec sandstone rock formations that appear to be on fire. Like Red Rock Canyon (*see earlier*), the park has scenic drives, hiking trails, and panoramic views. Its red, orange, and pink formations have appeared in several films, including *Viva Las Vegas* and *Total Recall*. Mouse's Tank Road is the main road through the park. Both entrances to the park are on Valley of Fire Highway, which runs along the southern part of the park. The visitor center is at the intersection of these two roads. At the center are exhibits on the geology, ecology, and history of the park and the surrounding area.

The park is open daily from sunrise to sunset. Temperatures are extreme in summer. The visitor center is open daily 9am-4pm. Tel. 702/397-2088. Admission to the park is $10 ($15 for non-Nevada vehicles). The park offers camping for $20 per night ($25 for non-Nevada residents), and visitors can make reservations through parks.nv.gov/parks/valley-of-fire. Some highlights of the park are:

• **Balanced Rock**: From the Visitor Center, you can stroll a short nature walk (.5 miles [.8 km]) to a rock formation with a rock balancing on top. You can even crawl inside of the rocks!

- **Rainbow Vista Trail**: This trail takes you on a 1.8-mile (2.9 km) loop past an explosion of colored rocks.
- **Mouse's Tank Trail**: The highlight of this .7 miles (1.1 km) trail takes you to rocks covered in petroglyphs (images created by removing part of a rock surface by incising, picking, or carving, as a form of rock art). You'll be looking at art that was created 4,000 years ago. To see more petroglyphs, climb the staircase at **Atlatl Rock**.
- **Fire Wave and Seven Wonders Trail**: Spectacular colored rock waves line this 1.5-mile (2.4 km) trail, making it one of the most popular in the park.
- **Petrified Logs Loop**: A short .3 mile (.5 km) trail that features petrified wood (the fossil of a tree that has been turned to stone). Informative panels explain the process.
- **Pastel (Pink) Canyon**: This scenic .4 mile (.64 km) walk takes you past remarkable rocks that are pastel pink.
- **White Domes Trail**: You'll find extraordinary views on this 1.1 mile (1.8 km) loop along with white and yellow sandstone formations. You can also visit the abandoned film set of the 1966 movie *The Professionals*.
- **Beehives**: These sandstone formations show how phenomenal designs are created by nature. Grooved lines, created over centuries, make the rocks look like large beehives.
- **Elephant Rock**: This rock formation, next to the east entrance, is said to resemble an elephant. It's a short .2 mile (.32 km) walk from the parking lot or you can stroll the 1.25 -mile (2 km) loop.

DEATH VALLEY

To reach Death Valley from Las Vegas, take Interstate 15 South to Nevada Highway 160 West. Drive 60 miles (97 km) to Pahrump, Nevada. Turn left on Bell Vista Road (three miles north of Highway 372). Drive 30 miles (48 km) to Death Valley Junction, California. Turn right onto California Highway 127 and then turn left on California Highway 190. Drive 30 miles (48 km) to the Visitor Center at Furnace Creek. The total trip is 120 miles (193 km). California Highway 190 is the main road through Death Valley. Some roads are damaged by Tropical Storm Hilary in August 2023.

When you think of Death Valley, you may think of meteorologists on television reporting that yet another record high temperature has been recorded in this unforgiving area of the desert. But Death Valley is so much more. Sure, there are extreme temperatures, but there are also wonders around every corner. From vast fields of wildflowers to the brilliant colors of the narrow canyon in the area known as Artist's Palette, you'll be amazed by the fabulous diversity of this remote part of California. Here are the highlights of your visit to this national park:

Furnace Creek
The main tourist information center is at Furnace Creek, with a small museum (featuring an informative 20-minute film), book store, detailed maps, and experienced and helpful park rangers. The center also offers snacks, sandwiches, and water. *Info:* CA-190, Tel 760/786-3200. Open daily. nps.gov/thingstodo/visit-the-furnace-creek-visitor-center.htm.

Also in Furnace Creek is the **Borax Museum** housed in a small building, the oldest structure in the park. Sodium borate, or borax, is only found here in the desert and in Turkey. Borax is a common laundry product used for more than 100 years. The museum is filled with artifacts from the borax mining era, and there are mining machines, antique wagons, carriages, and a steam locomotive outdoors. There are also exhibits highlighting the history of the area. The museum is part of the Oasis at Death Valley Hotel complex. *Info*: Off Highway 190 in Furnace Creek. Tel. 760/786-2345. Open daily. Admission: Free. www.oasisatdeathvalley.com.

Scotty's Castle
The only private mansion built in Death Valley is now a quirky museum. Albert Johnson and his wife Bessie were from Chicago and interested in life in Death Valley. They funded the construction of this strange structure in the middle of the desert. The Johnsons were friends with "Desert Valley Scotty," who many believed was a huckster who took advantage of anyone he met. Scotty (no one actually knows his real name) and the Johnsons used the castle as a venue to entertain everyone from Hollywood stars to presidents. Scotty claimed that his castle was built with money from his (nonexistent) gold mine. Tours take you through the castle and describe its interesting history. A highlight of your tour is the music room featuring a spectacular player organ. A bizarre and unusual experience. *Info*: Highway 267. Three miles (4.8 km) northeast of the intersection at Grapevine. Usually open daily. *Currently closed due to flood and fire damage.* www.nps.gov/deva/learn/historyculture/scottys-castle.htm.

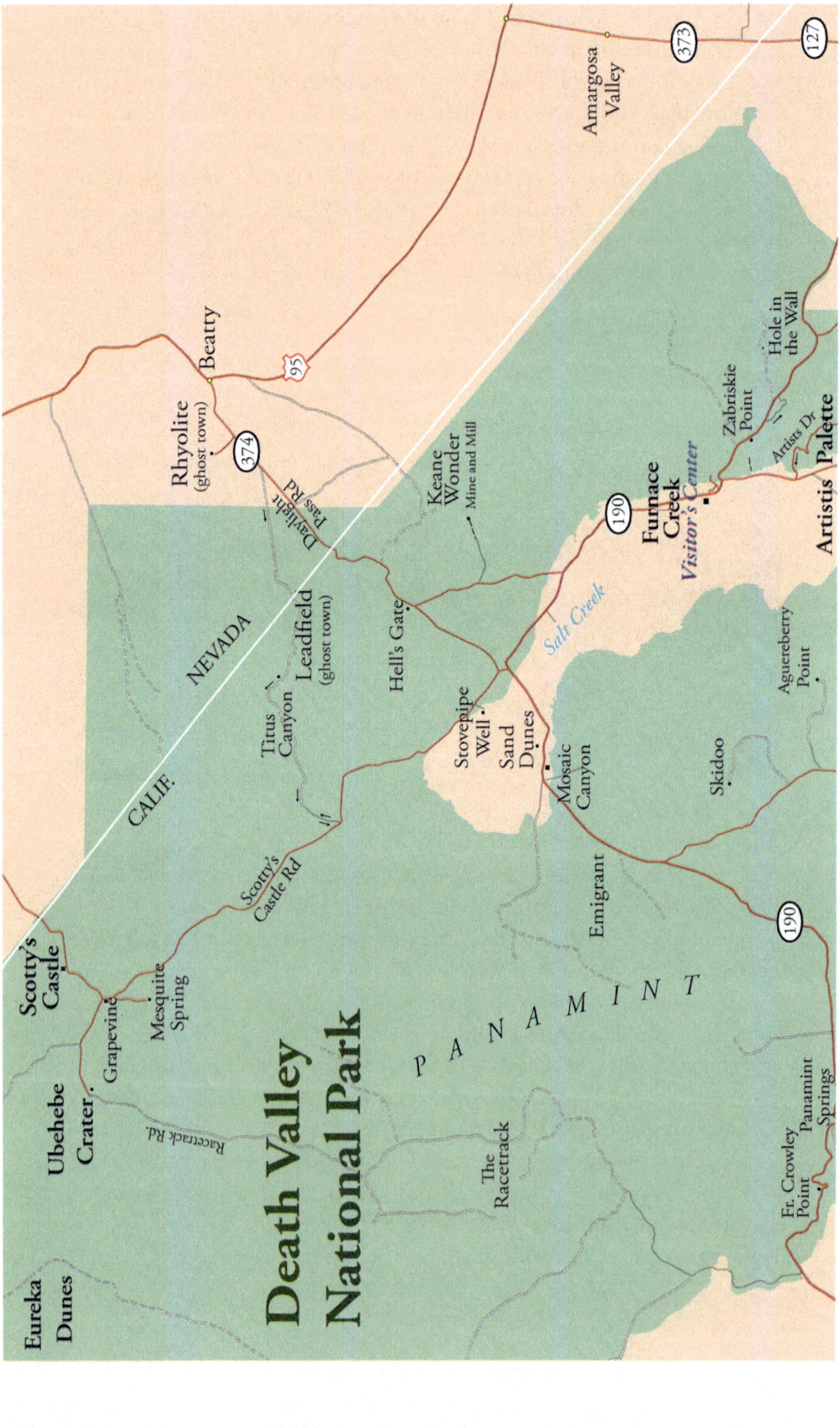

Death Valley National Park
Eureka Dunes
Ubehebe Crater
Racetrack Rd.
Grapevine
Scotty's Castle
Mesquite Spring
Scotty's Castle Rd
CALIF.
NEVADA
Titus Canyon
Leadfield (ghost town)
Daylight Pass Rd
374
Rhyolite (ghost town)
Beatty
95
Amargosa Valley
373
127
Hell's Gate
Keane Wonder Mine and Mill
Stovepipe Well
Sand Dunes
Mosaic Canyon
Salt Creek
190
Furnace Creek
Visitor's Center
Zabriskie Point
Hole in the Wall
Artists Dr
Artistis Palette
Aguereberry Point
Skidoo
Emigrant
P A N A M I N T
The Racetrack
Panamint Springs
Ft. Crowley Point

EXCURSIONS 77

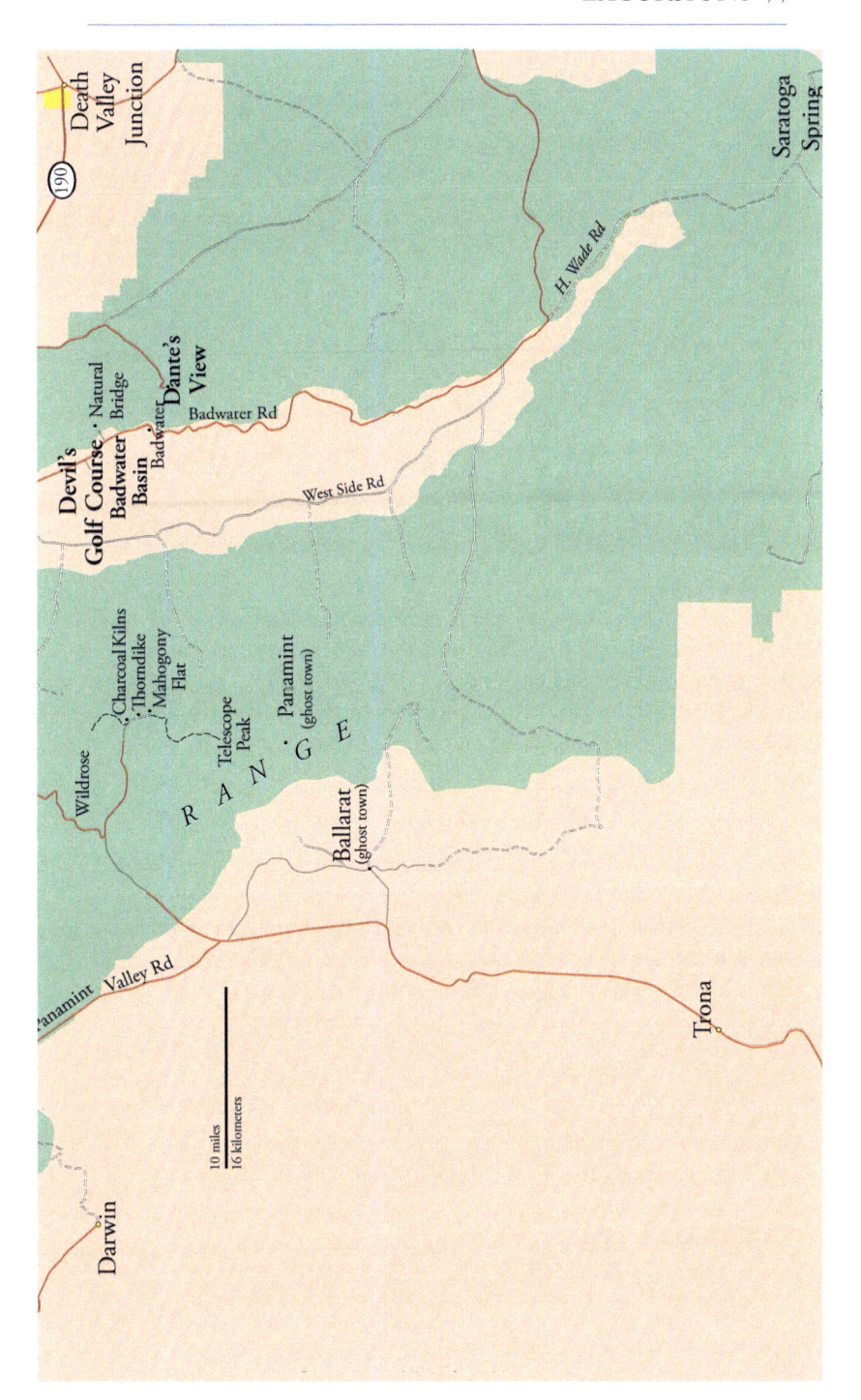

Artist's Palette
Don't miss this nine-mile (14.5 km) drive along a mountainside "painted" with brilliant colors. Metals have oxidized the clay, creating brilliant yellow, green, red, blue, and purple bands. There are plenty of turnoffs along the drive for you to take in the spectacular views of the basin. *Info*: Off Highway 178. Nine miles (14.5 km) south of Furnace Creek on Badwater Road.

Badwater Basin
This popular spot boasts the lowest point in North America at 282 feet (86 meters) below sea level. The salt flats here cover nearly 200 square miles (518 square km). Boardwalks take you over a spring-fed pond home to snails that are only found here. The shores of the pond are lined with salt-tolerant plants like pickleweed. This was once the site of ancient Lake Manly, which evaporated tens of thousands of years ago. The pond and salt flats are accessible from the parking lot off Badwater Road. You can also follow a two-mile (3.2 km) trail onto the salt flats (not recommended in the summer as the salt flats can be up to 80 degrees F [27 C] hotter than the air temperature). Look up to see the sign high above indicating sea level. *Info*: Badwater Road (17 miles/27 km) south of Furnace Creek.

Devil's Golf Course
This sprawling area of rock salt has been eroded by wind and rain into jagged spires. This was part of the ancient lake that once was here. If you

choose to walk here, be careful as the uneven surface is difficult to manage and the rocks and crystals are razor-sharp. If you do walk here, listen for the pops of tiny salt crystals bursting. Plaques describe the geology of the area. *Info*: Highway 178, 11 miles (17.7 km) southeast of Furnace Creek. The road to the parking lot is dirt.

Dante's View
At 5,475 feet (1,669 meters), this is the place to watch the sunset. Spectacular views of the entire Death Valley are worth the trip at any time of the day. *Info*: Off Highway 190, 10 miles (16 km) southeast of Furnace Creek.

Ubehebe Crater
In the northern part of Death Valley is this large volcanic crater. It was created over 300 years ago and is 600 feet (183 meters) deep and half a mile (.8 km) across. You can walk up to the edge of the crater and take in the black volcanic rock and colorful interior. The walk around the rim is about 1.5 miles (2.4 km) and takes you past several smaller craters, including Little Hebe. *Info*: From Highway 190, eight miles (13 km) west of Scotty's Castle near Grapevine.

Salt Creek
In the middle of Death Valley is a creek that is fed by small springs. You'll walk over boardwalks to protect the creek and the plants (especially pickleweed) that thrive here. The Death Valley pupfish live here in the creek and are found nowhere else in the world. An interesting experience to walk over a creek surrounded by vast desert. *Info*: Highway 190, 15 miles (24 km) north of Furnace Creek. The road from the highway to the creek is two miles (3.2 km) along a dirt road.

Eureka Dunes
The Eureka Dunes are northwest of Death Valley. These are some of the highest and largest dunes in North America, covering three square miles (4.8 km) and reaching 680 feet (24 meters) in places. The dry and windy weather can produce sounds that some have described as singing or whistling. *Info*: The remote dunes are located in northern Inyo County and accessible only by a gravel road from Grapevine Canyon to Big Pine in Owens Valley.

Sleeping and Eating in Death Valley
The Oasis at Death Valley $$$
Two distinct hotels make up this interesting complex. The historic Four Diamond Inn at Death Valley and the family-friendly Ranch at Death Valley both provide something for everyone. They feature a mineral pool, a spa, fine dining, a golf course, tennis courts, and horseback riding. *Info*: Off Highway 190 in Furnace Creek. Tel. 760/786-2345. Open daily. www.oasisatdeathvalley.com.

Amargosa Opera House and Hotel $$
New Yorker and dancer Marta Becker and her husband renovated this small theater in 1968. Marta painted elaborate murals on the ceiling and walls. She often performed here until her death in 2017 and performances are still held here. The adjoining adobe hotel was built between 1923 and 1925 to accommodate visiting investors of the mining companies. When mining left the area, the air-conditioned hotel was remodeled and opened to the public. Skylights brighten the rooms. The opera house and hotel were placed on the National Register of Historic Places in 1981, and Marta's murals are featured throughout the hotel. There's also a cafe. *Info*: Highway 127 and State Line Rd. in Death Valley Junction. Tel. 760/852-4441. www.amargosaoperahouse.org.

THE WORLD'S TALLEST THERMOMETER

This steel sign commemorates the weather record of 134°F (57°C) recorded in nearby Death Valley on July 10, 1913. In honor of that temperature record, the sign is 134 feet (41 meters) tall and the maximum temperature that it can record is 134°F (57°C). It had to be reinforced when high desert winds snapped it in half in 1992. Although it stopped working for a while, the family of Willis Herron (the builder of the monument) rescued and renovated this quirky sight. There's a touristy gift shop here. *Info*: 72157 Baker Blvd. in Baker, California. It's visible from Interstate 15. To reach Baker, California from Las Vegas, take Interstate 15 South for 93 miles (150 km). worldstallestthermometer.com.

82 LAS VEGAS MADE EASY

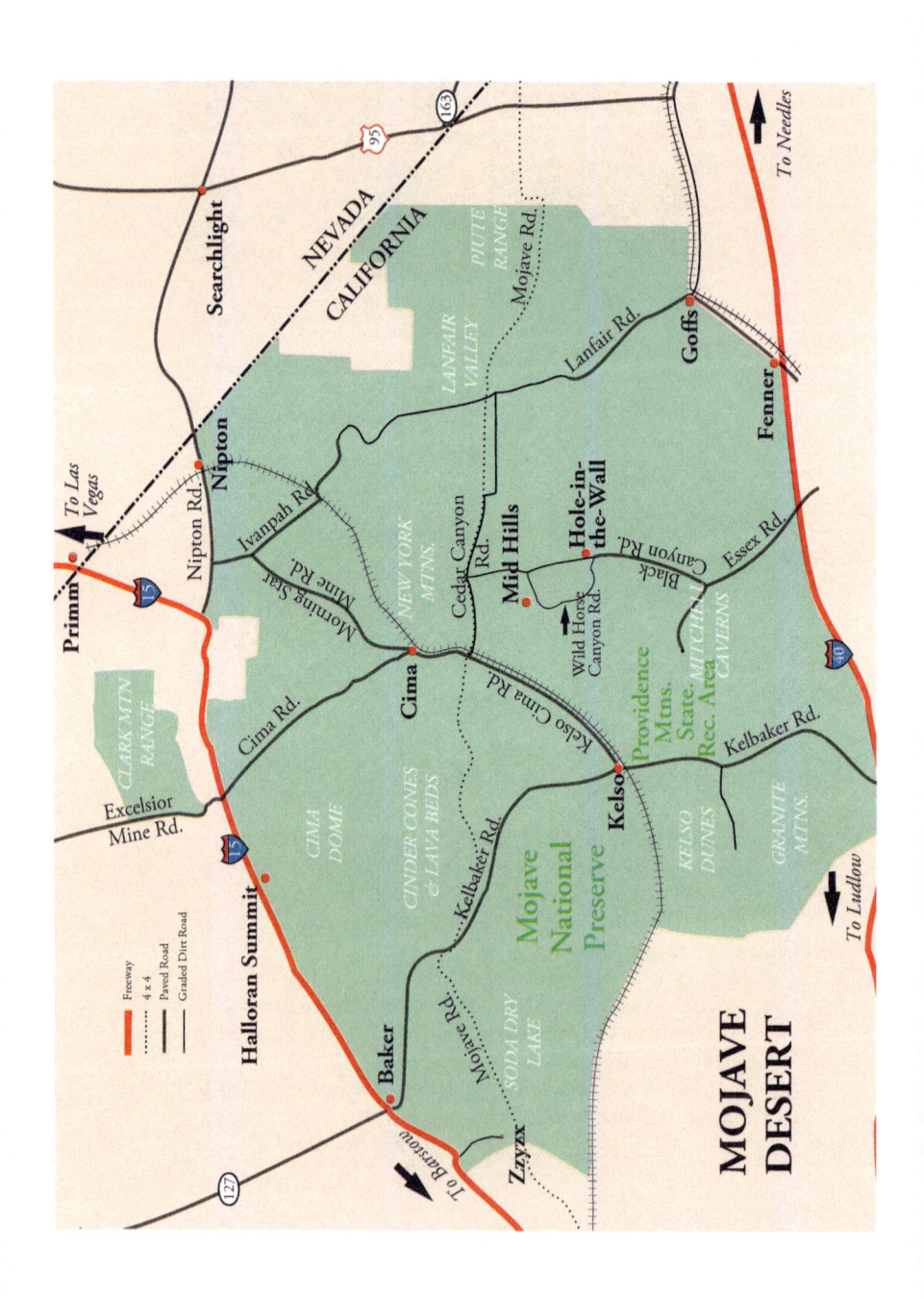

MOJAVE NATIONAL PRESERVE

The Mojave National Preserve is between Interstate 15 (to the north) and Interstate 40 (to the south). To reach Kelso, California, in the center of Mojave National Preserve, take Interstate 15 South for 93 miles (150 km) to California Highway 127 in Baker, California. Then take exit 246 and follow Kelbaker Road to Kelso Cima Road for 37 miles (60 km). Total trip is 130 miles (210 km). Some roads are damaged by Tropical Storm Hilary in August 2023.

What looks like miles and miles of barren land, the Mojave National Preserve is home to limestone caves (especially Mitchell Caverns), expansive sand dunes, ancient lava flows, and Joshua tree forests.

Kelso Depot

Originally opened in 1924 as a train station, the Spanish Mission Revival depot (*pictured above*) reopened in 2005 as the Visitor Center for Mojave National Preserve. The baggage room, ticket office, and dormitory rooms have been renovated to depict depot life during the first half of the 20th century. A small theater shows a short film on the preserve and history of the depot. But why is it located in the middle of nowhere? It was a necessary water stop for steam engine trains. It also served as a stop for passengers to refuel and for workers at nearby mines. To reach Kelso Depot from Interstate 15, exit at Kelbaker Road at Baker, and drive south 34 miles (54.7 km). From Interstate 40, exit Kelbaker Road (28 miles [48 km] east of Ludlow) and drive north 22 miles (35.4 km). *The visitor center is currently closed for renovations.*

Kelso Dunes

These massive dunes cover 45 square miles (72 square km) and are 600 feet tall (183 meters) at points. They're located just southwest of Kelso Depot and are the second-largest dune field in California. (The largest dune field is the Imperial Sand Dunes along Interstate 8 between the Imperial Valley and Arizona, just north of the Mexican border.) In spring, you can climb the dunes and take in the desert wildflowers.

Mitchell Caverns

Off Interstate 40, 56 miles (90 km) west of Needles, 116 miles (187 km) east of Barstow, and 16 miles (25.7 km) northwest of the Essex Road exit 100.

Mitchell Caverns are three spectacular limestone caves within the Providence Mountains State Recreation Area. The caverns are named after Jack Mitchell, who owned the tourist attraction from 1934 to 1954. These caves are the only limestone caves in the California State Park system. The "Tecopa" cave is named for a Shoshone Indian chief and "El Pakiva" cave means "Devil's House." They are connected by a man-made tunnel. Park rangers lead guided tours. The dangerous third cave, "Winding Stair" is closed to the public. Tours Fri-Sun by reservation only. *Info*: 38200 Essex Rd. in Essex. At the northwest end of Essex Rd., off Interstate 40. Tel. 760/928-2586.

stateparks.com/mitchell_caverns_state_park_in_california.html

Cima Dome
The summit of Cima Dome is 5,775 feet (1,755 meters). You can reach the top on a popular, and challenging, three-mile (five km) round-trip hike. You will be rewarded, as this is home to the world's largest concentration of Joshua trees. Sadly, in 2020 the Dome Fire burned 43,273 acres, and much of Cima Dome is now a graveyard of Joshua trees. Approximately 30% of the Joshua trees, nearly 1.3 million, were destroyed. Camping is available at the nearby Hole-in-the-Wall and Mid Hills campgrounds.

Rings Loop
The Rings Loop is a popular 1.5-mile (2.4 km) trail that takes you past ancient petroglyphs, and up a series of metal rings mounted in the rocks. This moderate hike is mostly flat until you reach the rings climb. The trail also connects to the Mid Hills to Hole-in-the-Wall Trail and the Barber Peak Trail.

MOJAVE MEMORIAL CROSS
What is a seven-foot-tall (2.1-meter) cross doing on a large boulder in the Mojave National Preserve? What about separation of church and state? A cross has been here since 1934 to commemorate fallen soldiers. It has been the subject of several court cases, including a decision by the U.S. Supreme Court, and a complicated land swap that resulted in it being on private land. It's been vandalized and even stolen, but now is looked after by the Veterans of Foreign Wars. *Info*: 12 miles (19.3 km) south of Interstate 15, east of Cima Dome.

ON THE NEVADA/CALIFORNIA BORDER
Primm

When driving to Las Vegas from California on Interstate 15, you'll pass through Primm, as you reach the Nevada/California border. The Primm Valley is home to three resorts: Whiskey Pete's, Primm Valley, and Buffalo Bill's. All three resorts have hotels and casinos. There's lots of free parking, charging stations, eateries, golf courses, and plenty of gambling options, from penny slots to roulette. The Star of the Desert Arena at Buffalo Bill's is an entertainment venue with seating for 6,500. The Bonnie and Clyde exhibit, at Buffalo Bill's, tells the history of their crime spree. It features the bullet-riddled vehicle that they were driving when police gunned them down in 1934 and Clyde's bloodstained death shirt. Also here is the Primm Mall (www.prizmoutlets.com) which has fallen on hard times and only a few stores remain. *Info*: Primm is 40 miles (64 km) southwest of Las Vegas on Interstate 15. www.primmvalleyresorts.com.

ON THE NEVADA/CALIFORNIA/ARIZONA BORDER
Laughlin

Laughlin is 90 miles (140 km) south of Las Vegas, at the southern tip of Nevada. Laughlin sits where Nevada, California, and Arizona meet. This resort town is the third most visited casino and resort destination in Nevada after Las Vegas and Reno. It's known for its cluster of casinos that include Harrah's, Golden Nugget, Tropicana, Aquarius, Edgewater, Laughlin River Lodge, The New Pioneer, and Don Laughlin's. Because of its location on the Colorado River, it's known for its water recreation activities and is one of the top destinations in the U.S. for Recreational Vehicles. Accommodations, entertainment, and dining in this laid-back river town are generally much cheaper than in Las Vegas.

www.visitlaughlin.com.

Hoover Dam and Lake Mead
To reach the Hoover Dam from Las Vegas, follow US 95 South to US 93 toward Boulder City. Total distance is 37 miles (60 km).

The impressive **Hoover Dam** (originally called the "Boulder Dam") was constructed during the Great Depression between 1931 and 1936 on the border of Nevada and Arizona. Over seven million people visit the site each year. The massive concrete dam is named after President Herbert Hoover and was dedicated by President Franklin D. Roosevelt. Such a large concrete structure had never been built before. Thousands of workers, many who were housed in nearby Boulder City, were involved in its construction, and over 100 of them lost their lives in the effort. The purpose of constructing the dam was to provide water, hydroelectric power, and control floods. Art Deco details add to the structure, especially the bronze angel sculptures, the "Winged Figures of the Republic."

Lake Mead is a reservoir formed by the dam on the Colorado River. It's the largest reservoir in the US in terms of water capacity. Also here is the world's tallest concrete arch bridge, the Mike O'Callaghan-Pat Tillman Memorial Bridge, towering over the dam. It connects Nevada and Arizona. If you're not squeamish about heights, you can walk along the bridge. The dam is a marvel of engineering. *Info*: Dam: Open daily 5am-9pm. Visitor Center: Open daily 9am-5pm (except Thanksgiving Day and Christmas Day). Tel. 702/494-2517 or 702/494-2901. Visitors can book guided dam tours and power plant tours through www.usbr.gov/lc/hooverdam/.

Grand Canyon's West Rim
To reach the West Rim from Las Vegas, take US route 95 South. US 95 South turns into US route 93 South before you reach Boulder City, Nevada. Continue for 77 miles (124 km) to Mohave County, Arizona. Exit on Pierce Ferry Rd. Continue to Diamond Bar Rd. for 49 miles (79 km) to the West Rim.

The majestic Grand Canyon is one of the most visited and awe-inspiring sights in the United States and the world. Layered bands of red rock reveal millions of years of geological history. The Colorado River cut its channels to create this monumental natural wonder. The Grand Canyon is 277 miles (446 km) long, 18 miles (29 km) wide, and over a mile deep (1,857 meters). Recent studies find the river has run through this area for about five to six million years, widening and deepening the canyon.

You can drive from The Strip to the West Rim of the Grand Canyon in a little over two hours. What a contrast between the neon lights and frenetic energy of Las Vegas and the scenic grandeur and quiet wonder of the Grand Canyon.

Any trip to the West Rim must include a visit to the cantilever glass bridge at Eagle Point. In 2007, the skywalk opened to the public. This modern engineering marvel took four years to build.

The 10-foot (3 meter) wide, horseshoe-shaped bridge has a glass bottom and extends over 70 feet (21 meters) over the Grand Canyon. The bridge is over 4,000 feet (1,219 meters) above the canyon floor. Not for those with a fear of heights! It's said to be strong enough to hold seventy fully loaded 747 passenger jets.

Also available from Eagle Point are helicopter tours, zipline, and rafting tours. *Info*: Open daily 8am-5pm. Admission: $68 (skywalk), $367 (skywalk, helicopter ride, pontoon ride). Other packages available at www.grandcanyonwest.com.

Pahrump
64 miles (103 km) via Nevada Route 160 West and Pahrump Valley Highway. www.visitpahrump.com.

You can come to Pahrump for its hotels, casinos, golfing, wild west countryside, and recreational vehicle rallies, but many come for another reason. Pahrump is famously, or infamously, known for its legal brothels. Two of the best known are Sheri's Ranch and the adjacent Chicken Ranch. Sheri's is a resort with tennis courts, a spa, swimming pool, and hotel. *Info*: www.sharisranch.com and www.chickenranchbrothel.com.

4. Sleeping and Eating

SLEEPING

Gambling, shows, attractions, and the bright neon lights might keep you up late in "Sin City," but you're going to have to sleep at some point! There is no shortage of options to sleep in Las Vegas. We've listed some of the major resorts along The Strip and downtown, and we've added some boutique hotels for you to consider. There's a room for you at all price points in Las Vegas.

Sleeping Prices

Prices for two people in a double room:
- $$$ over $200
- $$ $100-200
- $ under $100

The Strip
The Venetian Resort $$-$$$
The Venetian attempts to replicate the sights of Venice, including the Grand Canal, Rialto Bridge, St. Mark's Square, and the Doge's Palace. You can even take a gondola ride (*see page 23*). The hotel and casino complex opened in 1999 with over 4,000 rooms in its 35-story and 12-story towers. The sister property, **The Palazzo**, has its own hotel with 3,000 rooms and a casino. Within the famous resort, you will find multiple restaurants with celebrity chefs, lounges, sports betting, swimming pools, entertainment venues, and convention facilities. *Info*: 3355 S. Las Vegas Blvd. Tel. 702/414-4300. www.venetianlasvegas.com.

RESORT FEES

Before you celebrate that cheap rate you got for your room, check the resort fee. In the past, hotels may have added extra charges for using amenities, like the pool or gym. Now, the hotel adds a fee to your bill whether or not you use the amenities. Resort fees can be as much as the room rate. Almost all hotels on The Strip, and most downtown, have them. However, many hotels outside these areas do not.

Some argue that this violates Nevada law, but there is no current law that restricts these charges. You can ask for its removal at check-in, but it's highly unlikely that they will remove it. If you demand the removal, there is a risk that the hotel will cancel your reservation. Current resort fees run from $22 to $50 per night. And don't forget that you have taxes on top of all those charges.

Luxor $$

Among all the splashy resorts in Las Vegas, this resort, in the shape of a pyramid, is one of the most recognizable. You can visit New York City at the New York-New York Resort and Italy at the Venetian and Bellagio resorts, and you can take in Egypt at the Luxor. At 350 feet (107 meters) tall, the pyramid at the Luxor is almost as large as the ancient pyramids in Egypt. It's massive, with 30 stories, 4,400 guest rooms, casino, restaurants, spa, entertainment venues, and an enormous 19,000 square-foot pool. The Luxor features an ancient Egyptian theme and has the world's largest atrium. The tip of the pyramid features a light beam, which is said to be the most powerful man-made light in the world. For those not staying here, the best time to visit is at night when the pyramid is illuminated. *Info*: 3900 S. Las Vegas Blvd. luxor.mgmresorts.com.

Flamingo $$

This Las Vegas institution, with its iconic pink exterior, opened in 1946. It's one of the oldest resorts on The Strip. Mobster Bugsy Siegel built the hotel and casino, and he was murdered after it opened. It has seen expansion and renovation over the years and now has over 3,500 guest rooms. Among its attractions is the Wildlife Habitat, where you can roam four acres of gardens with waterfalls, winding streams, fish, exotic birds, and, of course, flamingos! *Info*: 3555 S. Las Vegas Blvd. www.caesars.com/flamingo-las-vegas/.

SLEEPING & EATING

New York-New York $$
Sure, Paris Las Vegas has its Eiffel Tower, but New York-New York has replicas of the Brooklyn Bridge, Statue of Liberty, and Empire State Building. The hotel features a roller coaster (*see page 19*), gourmet restaurants, and lively bars, all with a Big Apple vibe. *Info*: 3790 S. Las Vegas Blvd. www.newyorknewyork.com.

Resorts World $$-$$$
Resorts World is three resorts in one: Hilton, Conrad, and Crockfords. You can choose from 3,500 guest rooms spread over 66 floors. It's on the northern end of The Strip and one of the newest additions to the resort scene. There's an Asian theme here with pagodas, Koi ponds, and a massive gold lion at the entrance. The complex has over 40 restaurants, a casino, and a rooftop bar with an incredible view of the lights of The Strip. The Theatre at Resort World seats over 5,000 people and has hosted such notable entertainers as Celine Dion, Carrie Underwood, and Katy Perry. *Info*: 3000 S. Las Vegas Blvd. www.rwlasvegas.com.

Planet Hollywood $$
Hollywood in Las Vegas. You can stay in one of the over 2,500 movie-themed rooms at this resort in the center of The Strip. There's a lively casino, five bars, two pools, and 20 places to eat. *Info*: 3667 S. Las Vegas Blvd. www.caesars.com/planet-hollywood.

Excalibur $$
Inspired by Camelot and King Arthur, this theme hotel caters to families and has a large share of budget rooms. There's a massive pool, eight eateries, entertainment venues, and the Fun Dungeon with over 200 arcade and carnival games. *Info*: 3850 S. Las Vegas Blvd. www.excalibur.com.

Skylofts $$$
Take a dedicated elevator to your suite and get ready to be pampered at this boutique hotel on top of the MGM Grand. Concierge services include preferred seating at some of the best restaurants and shows in the city. Suites have two-story windows offering incredible views of The Strip. You'll have every amenity you can imagine at your fingertips. *Info*: 3799 S. Las Vegas Blvd. mgmgrand.mgmresorts.com/en/hotel/skylofts-mgm-grand.html.

94 LAS VEGAS MADE EASY

Paris Las Vegas $$
Pretend that you're wandering the streets of the City of Light at this resort with replicas of Paris attractions, including the Eiffel Tower. Just like Paris, there are plenty of gourmet dining options. There's also a rooftop pool, indoor mall, casino, eleven restaurants, and five bars. Rooms have French decor. *Info:* 3655 S. Las Vegas Blvd. www.caesars.com/paris-las-vegas.

Fontainebleau $$$
It took over 20 years to be completed, but it was worth the wait. This luxury hotel has 3,600 contemporary rooms, an impressive 150,000-square-foot casino, world-class dining, and entertainment and nightlife venues. Quite the addition to The Strip! *Info:* 2777 S. Las Vegas Blvd. www.fontainebleaulasvegas.com.

Mirage $$-$$$
Mirage seeks to create an oasis in the desert. When you check in, there's a gigantic aquarium with over 1,000 fish. The Polynesian theme continues through the hotel with swaying palm trees, waterfalls, and lush gardens. Don't miss the volcano eruption (*see page 31*). Plenty of dining and drinking options: *Info:* 3400 S. Las Vegas Blvd. www.mirage.com.

Caesars Palace $$
Enter the world of ancient Rome with opulent decor, gourmet dining, and exciting entertainment at the Colosseum stage. Although the hotel and casino are now over 50 years old, the hotel continues to undergo renovations and improvements, making it a favorite of repeat visitors. The boutique hotel at Caesars is **Nobu**. *Info:* 3570 S. Las Vegas Blvd. www.caesarspalace.com.

Mandalay Bay $$-$$$
One of the largest resorts on The Strip, this luxurious hotel has a tropical theme, amazing pool complex, shark reef (*see page 25*), and is a preeminent destination for live entertainment. Its House of Blues is one of the most popular venues for jazz and blues. **Delano** and **Four Season** are its boutique offerings. *Info:* 3950 S. Las Vegas Blvd. mandalaybay.mgmresorts.com/.

Cosmopolitan $$$
This hip and luxurious hotel has nearly 3,000 rooms with eight different room types to choose from. Most have balconies with sweeping views of The Strip. The "Cosmo" has a variety of dining options and chill bars. *Info*: 3708 S. Las Vegas Blvd. www.cosmopolitanlasvegas.com.

MGM Grand $$-$$$
The massive Grand has over 5,000 rooms and suites, 15 restaurants, and the Wet Republic Ultra Pool complex. Nine entertainment venues include the popular Hakkasan Nightclub. And, of course, there's a gigantic casino. The Grand's boutique hotel is **Signature**. *Info*: 3799 S. Las Vegas Blvd. mgmgrand.mgmresorts.com/.

MGM Park $$-$$$
MGM Park, formerly known as the Monte Carlo, is the smaller sister hotel to the adjacent MGM Grand. Even though it's a large hotel, it feels more intimate than the Grand. The upscale **Nomad**, a hotel-within-a-hotel, occupies nearly 300 of the Park's rooms. *Info*: 3770 S. Las Vegas Blvd. parkmgm.mgmresorts.com/.

Vdara $$$
The only completely non-smoking and non-gaming hotel in the city, this luxurious hotel is in a glass high rise in the CityCenter. You'll be pampered in its spa, complete with waterfall and meditation room. The studios have small kitchen areas. The pool has private retreats and cabanas with semi-secluded plunge pools. *Info*: 2600 W. Harmon Ave. vdara.mgmresorts.com.

Aria $$$
The Aria is on The Strip, but set back farther than some the others. This luxury resort and casino, in the CityCenter complex, has two curved glass towers, rising 50 stories. The hotel has over 4,000 rooms and suites. Its rooms are immense, all over 500 square feet (46 meters). *Info*: 3730 S. Las Vegas Blvd. aria.mgmresorts.com.

Waldorf Astoria $$$
This non-gaming hotel, formerly the Mandarin Oriental, has nearly 400 luxury rooms and suites. The 47-story tower is also home to over 200 opulent condominiums. Want to do some high-end shopping? Take the sky bridge to the Shops at Crystals. *Info*: 3752 S. Las Vegas Blvd. www.hilton.com/en/brands/waldorf-astoria/.

TIME TO DRINK!

The alcohol flows freely in "Sin City." You'll have no problem finding a place to imbibe. Here are a few places where you can chug a beer, savor a glass of wine, sip a craft cocktail, or tilt your head back and down a shot.

Allē Lounge on 66

With stunning views of the neon lights of The Strip, this lounge on the top floor of Resorts World is known for its handcrafted cocktails and small plates. *Info*: 3000 S. Las Vegas Blvd. www.rwlasvegas.com.

Chandelier

The Cosmopolitan Hotel is home to this three-story lounge dominated by a massive chandelier. *Info*: 3708 S. Las Vegas Blvd. www.cosmopolitanlasvegas.com/lounges-bars/the-chandelier.

Skyfall

Take in the views of Las Vegas from the 64th floor of the Delano Hotel. *Info*: 3940 S. Las Vegas Blvd. delanolasvegas.mgmresorts.com/en/nightlife/skyfall-lounge.html.

Gilley's

Ride a mechanical bull or line dance to country music at this saloon, dance hall, and BBQ inside the Treasure Island Hotel & Casino. *Info*: 3300 S. Las Vegas Blvd. gilleyslasvegas.com.

Atomic Liquors

Opened in 1952, this is the oldest free-standing bar in Las Vegas. The downtown bar has been featured in movies like *The Hangover* and *Casino*. The Rat Pack cavorted here (and so did Barbra Streisand). *Info*: 917 E Fremont St. www.atomic.vegas.

Peppermill Restaurant and Fireside Lounge

Featured in the films *Showgirls* and *Casino*, this restaurant and bar opened in 1972. Rat Pack members, especially Dean Martin, Jerry Lewis, and Joey Bishop, drank many tiki cocktails here, under its neon lights. *Info*: 2985 S. Las Vegas Blvd. www.peppermilllasvegas.com.

Minus5°

Get ready for some relief from the brutal Las Vegas heat at this ice bar. Even the glasses are made of ice! A warm wrap is provided to keep you from freezing. *Info*: Three locations include Mandalay Bay, LINQ Promenade, and Grand Canal Shoppes at the Venetian. minus5experience.com.

SLEEPING & EATING

Wynn & Encore $$$
This is the largest five-star resort in the world. Wynn offers luxurious accommodations, world-class dining at restaurants helmed by celebrity chefs, live concerts, shopping at the upscale Wynn Esplanade, spa, several pools, and a sprawling casino. There's even a golf course here, where golfers walk under a waterfall to get to the 18th hole. The Encore Theater is between the two resorts. It seats 1,500 people and has hosted diverse entertainers, such as Beyoncé and Garth Brooks. *Info*: 3131 S. Las Vegas Blvd. www.wynnlasvegas.com.

The STRAT $$
Formerly known as the Stratosphere, the STRAT is a hotel, casino, and tower on the north end of The Strip. Soaring 1,149 feet (350 meters), this is the tallest observation tower in the country. Dine or have a drink on the observation deck and enjoy incredible views of Las Vegas. *Info*: 2000 Las Vegas Blvd. South. www.thestrat.com.

LINQ $$
LINQ has an excellent location in the center of The Strip. Contemporary rooms, diverse dining options, multiple bars, and a vibrant casino are all available for the guest. Also here is the High Roller, the largest observation wheel in North America, and shopping at the LINQ Promenade. *Info*: 3535 S. Las Vegas Blvd. www.caesars.com/linq.

Palms $$-$$$
The Palms is an underrated hotel located off The Strip. It has been recently renovated and is now owned by the San Manuel Band of Mission Indians. The resort is popular with a youngish crowd. The property offers fine dining, a casino, rooftop bars, and is renowned for its world-class art collection. *Info*: 43121 W. Flamingo Rd. www.palms.com.

CityCenter

CityCenter is the most expensive privately funded project in the U.S. It was designed to be a "city within a city" and sits at a prime location on The Strip. It's known for its unique architecture, including the metal-and-glass exterior of the building housing the Shops at Crystals. There are five properties here: Vdara Hotel, Aria Resort, Waldorf Astoria, Veer Towers (a residential community), and the Shops at Crystals. The CityCenter also has a casino, luxury spas, and modern art displayed throughout the complex. *Info*: 3740 S. Las Vegas Blvd.

Cromwell $$

The only "boutique hotel" on The Strip has 188 Parisian-inspired rooms. There's a casino, club, and eateries, including the popular Giada, run by Giada De Laurentiis. Its location is convenient to explore nearby attractions such as The High Roller observation wheel, LINQ shopping promenade, and the fountains at the Bellagio. *Info*: 3595 S. Las Vegas Blvd. www.caesars.com/cromwell.

Circus Circus $$

It has seen better days, but Circus Circus is a fun destination for families. There are free circus acts nightly, a carnival Midway, and The Adventuredome with over 25 rides, including a double-loop rollercoaster (*see page 24*). *Info*: 2880 S. Las Vegas Blvd. www.circuscircus.com.

Bally's $$

Bally's is an affordable option with a central location on The Strip. There are several swimming pools, shopping areas, and tennis courts. A bonus is access to the amenities at the connected, and fancier, Paris Las Vegas. *Info*: 3645 S. Las Vegas Blvd. www.ballylasvegas.com.

SLEEPING & EATING

Sahara $$
The Sahara is on the north end of The Strip between Circus Circus and the STRAT. The hotel is in the mid-range of prices and amenities. There's an expansive casino, several restaurants at all price points, live music and performance venues, spa, and three comfortable pools. *Info*: 2535 S. Las Vegas Blvd. www.saharalasvegas.com.

Downtown
Circa $$-$$$
This resort and casino opened in 2020. It's downtown on the Fremont Street Experience and is the first new building constructed in the area since 1980. Las Vegas Club, Mermaids Casino, and the Glitter Gulch strip club were all demolished to make way for the 35-story tower. The lobby displays the former Vegas Vickie cowgirl neon sign, which was once used at the strip club. Across the street is a nine-story parking garage known as Garage-Mahal. There's a two-story casino and a sportsbook. The three-story sportsbook is where can wager on sports competitions, including football (the Super Bowl is the largest game for betting), baseball, basketball, hockey, soccer, horse racing, greyhound racing, and fighting events. Stadium Swim has six pools over three levels, private cabanas, day beds, chaise lounge chairs, swim-up bars and a gigantic 143-foot screen broadcasting sporting events (*see photo above*). *Info*: 8 Fremont St. Tel. 702/247-2258. www.circalasvegas.com.

Golden Nugget $-$$
You might feel you have stepped back in time at this historic downtown hotel and casino. Classic accommodations, a lively casino, and "The Tank," a tropical oasis with a large swimming pool, a shark tank with a water slide that passes through it, and private cabanas for rent. *Info*: 129 E. Fremont St. www.goldennugget.com/las-vegas.

SHOWS

Las Vegas draws the biggest names in entertainment, and it also has some of the most spectacular stage shows. Here are a few of the long-running shows that continue to thrill visitors.

The Beatles LOVE

Cirque du Soleil at the Mirage stages a theatrical production that showcases the music of The Beatles.
www.cirquedusoleil.com/beatles-love.

O

Another Cirque du Soleil production with a water theme is staged at the Bellagio. Seven hydraulic lifts change the water level for incredible diving and swimming acrobatics.
www.cirquedusoleil.com/o.

KÀ

The MGM Grand is home to this Cirque du Soleil production. KÀ tells the tale of twins on a journey to fulfill their destiny. The sumptuous production features martial arts, pyrotechnics, and aerial acrobatics. www.cirquedusoleil.com/ka.

Terry Fator

Long-running performance at The Mirage, featuring ventriloquist Terry Fator, puppets, live music, and celebrity impressions.
terryfator.com.

Mystère
Get ready to have your senses overwhelmed at this production by Cirque du Soleil at Treasure Island. You'll experience dramatic dancing, amazing costumes, thrilling acrobatics, and innovative lighting. www.cirquedusoleil.com/mystere.

Absinthe
A theater-in-the-round at Caesars Palace is home to this adults-only show. It's a blend of burlesque, acrobatics, and comedy. Audience participation plays a large role in the production. spiegelworld.com/shows/absinthe/.

Penn & Teller
You might get asked to join this duo on stage at this dynamic magic show with audience participation. They're known for revealing the secrets of their magic tricks to the audience at the Rio Hotel and Casino. pennandteller.com/tickets/.

Blue Man Group
An elaborate stage at the Luxor is home to blue-skinned performers. The production features electronic, rock, and pop music. Group members play a variety of instruments, including custom-made pipe and percussion instruments. www.bluemangroup.com.

Tournament of Kings
The tale of King Arthur and his knights is told at this theater at the Excalibur. This long-running show features knights on their horses who joust with the aid of special effects and pyrotechnics. While the knights fight, you dine using your hands as utensils. www.mgmresorts.com/en/entertainment/excalibur/tournament-of-kings.html

Michael Jackson- One
This Cirque du Soleil production at The Mandalay Bay Theatre honors the career of Michael Jackson, the "King of Pop." www.cirquedusoleil.com/michael-jackson-one.

HANG OUT WITH LOCALS

Las Vegas is one of the fastest growing metropolitan areas in the U.S. Many who live here avoid The Strip and instead hang out and gamble at resorts and casinos that cater to those who live and work in Las Vegas.

While not as glitzy as those downtown and on The Strip, these are good places to eat, drink, play, and have a "staycation."
- **Red Rock Canyon**: *Info*: 11011 W. Charleston Blvd. www.redrockresort.com.
- **Santa Fe Station**: 4949 N. Rancho Dr. www.santafestation.com.
- **Durango**: 6915 S. Durango Dr. www.durangoresort.com.

Four Queens $-$$
Located downtown on Fremont Street, the Four Queens Hotel offers a classic Las Vegas experience, a casino, on-site dining, and a rooftop pool. The Canyon Club is a popular venue for live music and comedy shows. Step out of the lobby, take in the retro neon signs, and stroll down the vibrant Fremont Street Experience. *Info*: 202 Fremont St. www.fourqueens.com.

Downtown Grand $$
No circus or King Arthur theme at this modern hotel. You'll be a few blocks away from the Fremont Street Experience and other downtown attractions. There's a casino and several restaurants and bars. Sit in the hot tub at the rooftop Citrus Grand Pool Deck and take in the panoramic views of downtown Las Vegas. *Info*: 206 N. 3rd St. www.downtowngrand.com.

Las Vegas Hostel $
If you're counting your pennies, or just don't want to spend a lot on your accommodations, you can stay at the only Las Vegas hostel with a swimming pool. Shared rooms start at $27, but there are also private rooms available. Amenities include breakfast, backpack-sized lockers, day storage, bicycles, and parking. *Info*: 1322 Fremont St. lasvegashostel.net.

Further Afield
Red Rock Casino, Hotel, & Spa $$
Red Rock is away from the hustle and bustle, just ten miles (16 km) west of The Strip. It's nestled at the gateway to the gorgeous Red Rock Canyon. Newly renovated rooms, dining options, and a lively casino all await you. Red Rock has the finest pool off The Strip with fabulous views of the red rocks in the distance. It also has a 72-lane bowling center with fog machines and lighting effects. *Info*: 11011 W. Charleston Blvd. Driving distance from The Strip is 11 miles (17.7 km). Tel.702/797-7777. www.redrockresort.com.

The Platinum Hotel and Spa $$
Just one block away from The Strip, The Platinum Hotel offers all-suite accommodations with full kitchens. This is a non-gaming and non-smoking facility. The hotel has modern decor and a rooftop pool. *Info*: 211 E. Flamingo Rd. www.theplatinumhotel.com.

Eating Prices

Prices for a main course:
- $$$$ Very Expensive: over $30
- $$$ Expensive: $21-$30
- $$ Moderate: $10-$20
- $ Inexpensive: under $10

EATING
You may think of bargain buffets with mediocre food when you think of dining in Las Vegas, but you shouldn't. From restaurants with celebrity chefs to Rat Pack haunts, you'll find something for every diner in the city. And, we'll also tell you where to get good food at those famous buffets.

Casa Di Amore $$-$$$
Candle lit tables, photo art depicting old Vegas, and live Rat Pack music all make Casa Di Amore a fine choice for dining. The theme here is "Las Vegas, the way it used to be." The menu features Italian dishes like osso bucco, cioppino, lasagna, chicken Marsala, and veal parmigiana. Down it all with a classic cocktail or the decent house Chianti. End your meal with a cannoli, pastry filled with sweet cream and ricotta cheese. Waiters who have served the clientele for years add to the experience. *Info*: 2850 E. Tropicana Ave.. Tel. 702/433-4967. Open Thu-Mon 11am-4am. casadiamore.com.

Mon Ami Gabi $$-$$$
This traditional French bistro is in the Paris Las Vegas Resort. You'll dine on classic French fare like *steak frites* and onion soup. For breakfast, try the waffles or French toast. At lunch, have the *croque monsieur* (ham, gruyere cheese, and mornay sauce). French wines are served by the glass or the bottle from a rolling wine cart. Fabulous outdoor patio. *Info*: 3655 S. Las Vegas Blvd. Tel. 702/944-4224. Open Sun-Thu 7am-10pm (Fri and Sat until 11pm). monamigabi.com.

Top of the World $$$$
You'll have sweeping views of the city at this restaurant 800 feet (244 meters) above The Strip at The STRAT Hotel. The restaurant revolves 360 degrees every 80 minutes. You'll pay for the view, but the award-winning restaurant serves fine dining in an elegant atmosphere. Your choices likely will include a rack of lamb, a shellfish tower, and roasted lobster tail. *Info*: 2000 S. Las Vegas Blvd. Tel. 800/789-9436. Open daily 4pm-11pm. Upscale dress code. thestrat.com/restaurants/top-of-the-world

Taverna Costera $$
The Las Vegas Arts District is home to this casual, fun restaurant. The menu features Mediterranean fusion dishes with Spanish, French, Italian, and Greek cuisines. Start with *Iberico jamon croquetas* (deep fried Iberico ham with mango jelly) and for your main course, try the Mediterranean Orzo Bowl or Chicken Katsu Curry Plate. Also here is Dragon's Alley Coffee, a rooftop bar, and live entertainment and event space. *Info*: 1031 S. Main St. Tel. 702/749-0091. Wed-Fri 11am-10pm, Sat 10am-10pm Sun 10am-9pm. tavernacostera.com.

Eiffel Tower Restaurant $$$$
You're not in Paris, France, but the food will sure make you think you are. Take in the splendid views of The Strip while dining in a replica of the Eiffel Tower. Start with *foie gras* and dine on roasted free range chicken with wild mushrooms or filet mignon with béarnaise sauce. Excellent French wine list. *Info*: 3655 S. Las Vegas Blvd. Tel. 702/948-6937. Open daily 5pm-10pm, Fri-Sun brunch 10am-2pm. www.eiffeltowerrestaurant.com.

CHINATOWN
Walk through the traditional Chinese entrance gate, take in the pagoda-style roofs, and get ready to explore Asian Cuisine. There are Chinese, Filipino, Korean, Japanese, and Vietnamese restaurants all within a small area. *Info*: 4255 Spring Mountain Rd. www.lvchinatownplaza.com.

Triple George Grill $$-$$$
There are a lot of steak houses in Las Vegas, but this one downtown feels like you have stepped back in time. Begin your dinner with a tasty Caesar salad, followed by a hearty steak with two sides, and finish it all off with a slice of cheesecake. "George" is slang for an all-around good guy (and big tipper). *Info*: 201 N. Third St. Tel. 702/384-2761. Open Mon-Fri for lunch, daily for dinner 4pm-close. www.triplegeorgegrill.com.

Anima $$$-$$$$
This spot takes its name from the Spanish and Italian word for "soul." Innovative dishes from Spain and Italy are served at this modern eatery located off The Strip. Try the oysters, eggplant parmigiana, or sea bass with fennel. There are separate vegetarian, vegan, and gluten-free menus. It's known for its wine list featuring selections from small producers. *Info*: 9205 W. Russell Rd. Unit 18, (702)-202-4291. Open daily 5pm-9pm. animabyedo.com.

Sickies Garage Burgers & Brews $$
This garage-theme restaurant and bar, complete with classic vehicles hanging from the ceiling, is a casual and fun destination. The family-friendly eatery, at Town Square Park on the south end of The Strip, serves 50 different burgers and 50 beers. Also on the menu are shakes, wings, and fish and chips. It's a good place to watch sports. *Info*: 6629 S. Las Vegas Blvd. Tel. 725/735-5400. Open Mon-Thu 11am-10am, Fri 11am-midnight, Sat 10am-midnight, Sun 10am-10pm. sickiesburgers.com/locations/las-vegas/.

SkinnyFATS $-$$
Not sure if you want to eat healthy or be naughty? SkinnyFATS, with four locations in greater Las Vegas, divides its menu into lower calorie choices and "happy" choices that are higher in calories. So you can choose a rice bowl and feel good about yourself or a Cowboy Candy burger, with cheese and candied jalapeños, and be super full. *Info*: 6261 Dean Martin Dr. Tel. 702/979-9797. Open daily 10am-8pm. skinnyfats.com.

Beerhaus $$
This beer hall has a great location in the pedestrian area next to Park MGM, New York-New York, and the T-Mobile Arena. Extensive selection of beer, cocktails, and wine. It's a favorite gathering place before events at T-Mobile Arena, home to the Vegas Golden Knights NHL team. The kitchen dishes out sandwiches like the brisket sandwich and black bean burger. So, grab a cold brew and hang out on the large outdoor patio. *Info*: 3790 S. Las Vegas Blvd. Tel. 702/692-2337. Open daily at 10am. newyorknewyork.mgmresorts.com/en/restaurants/beerhaus.html

CELEBRITY CHEFS

Celebrity chef restaurants are all the rage in Las Vegas. Here are some of the most notable ones and their locations.

Giada
This restaurant, at the Cromwell, is owned by celebrity chef Giada De Laurentiis and offers Italian-inspired cuisine with modern twists and stunning views of The Strip. *Info*: 3595 S. Las Vegas Blvd. www.giadadelaurentiis.com/restaurants.

Gordon Ramsay Hell's Kitchen
At Caesars Palace, this restaurant offers a menu inspired by the popular television show "Hell's Kitchen," featuring dishes created by celebrity chef Gordon Ramsay. *Info*: 3570 S. Las Vegas Blvd. www.gordonramsayrestaurants.com.

Joël Robuchon
The legendary French chef Joël Robuchon helms this fine dining establishment at the MGM Grand and offers exquisite French cuisine in an elegant setting. *Info*: 3799 S. Las Vegas Blvd. jrobuchon.com/restaurants/las-vegas.

Bobby Flay's Mesa Grill
Caesars Palace is home to this restaurant by Bobby Flay, known for its Southwestern-inspired cuisine and vibrant atmosphere. *Info*: 3570 S. Las Vegas Blvd. www.mesagrill.com.

Emeril's New Orleans Fish House
At the MGM Grand, this restaurant is by Emeril Lagasse, offering a menu of fresh seafood and Creole-inspired dishes in a lively setting. *Info*: 3799 S. Las Vegas Blvd. emerilsrestaurants.com.

Spago
Wolfgang Puck's restaurant at the Bellagio offers California cuisine with global influences in a stylish setting. *Info*: 3600 S. Las Vegas Blvd. wolfgangpuck.com/restaurants/spago-las-vegas.

Craftsteak
Tom Colicchio (co-founder of the Gramercy Tavern in New York City) serves high-quality steaks and seasonal dishes prepared with locally sourced ingredients, at the MGM Grand. *Info*: 3799 S. Las Vegas Blvd. www.craftsteaklasvegas.com.

Guy Fieri's Vegas Kitchen & Bar
The LINQ Hotel features this restaurant offering a casual dining experience with bold flavors and comfort food classics. *Info*: 3535 S. Las Vegas Blvd. www.guyfieri.com.

The Bedford
The Bedford by Martha Stewart at Paris Las Vegas is a replica of Martha's 1925 farmhouse, with culinary inspiration drawn from her love of French cooking. *Info*: 3655 S. Las Vegas Blvd. www.caesars.com/paris-las-vegas.

Nobu
Chef Nobu Matsuhisa is a world-renowned sushi chef. At Caesars Palace, you can feast on imported Asian and Japanese fish, seafood, and exotic delicacies. There's also vegan, vegetarian, and gluten-free options. *Info*: 3570 S. Las Vegas Blvd. noburestaurants.com.

Mr. Chow
Michael Chow opened the first Mr. Chow in 1968, offering authentic Beijing cuisine. The restaurant, at Caesars Palace, became an international sensation. *Info*: 3570 S. Las Vegas Blvd. www.mrchow.com.

Guy Savoy
Guy Savoy's restaurant at Caesars Palace serves elegant French cuisine in a fine dining environment. It's designed to emulate the menu of his Paris restaurant. *Info*: 3570 S. Las Vegas Blvd. www.guysavoy.com.

Dominique Ansel
French pastry chef Dominique Ansel is best known for his invention of the Cronut, a croissant-donut hybrid. Try it, and other delicious pastries, at this shop at Caesars Palace. *Info*: 3570 S. Las Vegas Blvd. www.dominiqueansel.com.

PizzaCake
PizzaCake by *Cake Boss* star Buddy Valastro, recreates the typical New Jersey/New York-style pizzeria, at Harrah's. *Info*: 3475 S. Las Vegas Blvd. www.pizzacake.com.

Las Vegas is renowned for its **buffet** offerings, with hotels and casinos featuring elaborate spreads. Here are some of the best buffets in Las Vegas:

Bacchanal Buffet at Caesars Palace: Regarded as one of the best buffets in Las Vegas, Bacchanal Buffet offers a vast selection of dishes from around the world, including seafood, sushi, and prime rib. The buffet features several live cooking stations. *Info*: 3570 S. Las Vegas Blvd. www.caesars.com/caesars-palace/restaurants. From $32.99.

Wicked Spoon at The Cosmopolitan: Known for its upscale and inventive approach to buffet dining, Wicked Spoon offers a diverse array of dishes presented in individual servings and small plates. Guests can enjoy everything from gourmet salads and *charcuterie* to carved meats and decadent desserts. *Info*: 3708 S. Las Vegas Blvd. www.cosmopolitanlasvegas.com/restaurants/wicked-spoon. From $47.

The Buffet at Wynn: This buffet has earned a reputation for its elegant atmosphere and gourmet offerings. Guests can indulge in a wide range of dishes, including fresh seafood, sushi, pasta, and desserts, all prepared with the quality ingredients. *Info*: 3131 S. Las Vegas Blvd. From $38.99. www.wynnlasvegas.com/dining/casual-dining/the-buffet. From $54.99.

The Buffet at Bellagio: Guests can enjoy a variety of dishes, including seafood, prime rib, Italian specialties, and an extensive dessert selection, all presented in a luxurious dining environment. *Info*: 3600 S. Las Vegas Blvd. bellagio.mgmresorts.com/en/restaurants/the-buffet.html. From $66.

Circus Buffet: Comfort food classics are served at Circus Circus at a reasonable price point. It's family-friendly, and kids under three eat free. *Info*: 2880 S. Las vegas Blvd. From $20. www.circuscircus.com/restaurants-1/.

5. Planning Your Trip/Practical Matters

Arriving/Getting Around
Harry Reid International Airport (LAS), formerly known as McCarran International Airport, is five miles (8 km) south of downtown Las Vegas. Its location makes it convenient for travelers to get to where they are staying. www.harryreidairport.com. Look at all those slot machines! You can get an early start on gambling upon arrival, or you can spend some time waiting for your flight winning or losing some more money.

Taxis
If you want to take a taxi from the airport, follow the signs leading to Level Zero, near exit door #52. A taxi ride from the airport to downtown and The Strip is around $25.

Rideshare
The rideshare pickup location for Terminal 1 is on Level 2 of the T1 Parking Garage. From Baggage Claim, take the elevator near Door 2 up to Level 2, cross the pedestrian bridge to the parking garage, and the pickup area is to the right. Rideshare pickup for Terminal 3 is on the Valet Level of the T3 Parking Garage. Pay attention to your driver's instructions, as they will provide you with a specific parking lane. Attend to the guard's instructions.

Car Rental
All major car-rental companies operate at LAS. Follow signs for Ground Transportation, exit the building, and proceed to the Rental Car Shuttle pickup area. Free shuttle buses run between the airport terminals and the Rental Car Center.

Bus
The Regional Transportation Commission (www.rtcsnv.com) runs the *Deuce on The Strip* line, which is a 24-hour bus line that goes from the South Strip Transit Terminal up to the Fremont Street Experience in downtown Las Vegas. There are multiple stops along The Strip, including locations where you can connect with the Las Vegas Monorail (*see below*). A single ride is $4, two hour pass $6, 24-hour pass $8, and three-day pass $20. You can purchase tickets on the bus, at ticket vending machines, and through the rideRTC app.

The **Greyhound Bus Station** is located at the Las Vegas S Strip Transit Terminal at 6675 Gilespie St.

Monorail
The **Monorail** trains (www.lvmonorail.com) arrive every four to eight minutes at stations along The Strip, with stops at all major resorts. Station hours are Mon 7am-midnight, Tue-Thu 7am-2am, Fri-Sun 7am-3am. A single ride is $6, day pass $15, week pass $62. Passengers can purchase tickets at vending machines at the stations. Mobile tickets can be purchased online at a discount. The seven stops on the route are:
- SAHARA Station
- Westgate Station
- Boingo Station at Las Vegas Convention Center
- Harrah's/The LINQ Station
- Flamingo/Caesars Palace Station
- Horseshoe/Paris Station
- MGM Grand Station.

GoCar Tours
Hop in a little yellow car and tour the iconic sights of Las Vegas at your own pace. GPS guides you to the sights with informative, and funny, commentary. Not your typical tour bus experience. *Info*: 723 S. Casino Blvd. (in the Arts District). From $149.99 (two hours). Reservations at gocartours.com.

Practical Matters
Banking & Money
Call your credit-card company or bank before you leave to tell them you'll be using your ATM or credit card outside your usual area. Many have automatic controls that can "freeze" your account if the computer program determines that there are charges outside your normal range. ATMs (with fees, of course) are the easiest way to change money if you are visiting from outside the United States. You'll find them everywhere, including the airport.

Cannabis
Adults 21 and older may now buy marijuana products in Nevada, regardless of whether they are a Nevada citizen. All you need is identification, such as a driver's license or a state-issued identification card. You may consume at a private residence, but not in public. So, no walking down The Strip smoking a joint! **Planet 13** bills itself as the world's largest dispensary, with

dining, bar, and retail. There's also a smoking area called "Dazed! Lounge." *Info*: 2548 W. Desert Inn Rd. Suite 100. Tel. 702/815-1313. Open 24 hours daily with curbside pickup and delivery.www.planet13lasvegas.com.

Climate & Weather

Summers are sweltering, the winters can be cold, and it is dry and mostly clear year round. The hottest month of the year is July, with an average high of 104°F (40°C) and a low of 80°F (26.7°C). The coolest month of the year is December, with an average low of 39°F (2.2°C) and a high of 58°F (14.4°C).

Average high temperature/low temperature °F and °C and days of rain:

High °F	Low °F		High °C	Low °C	Rainfall (inches)
59	39	January	15	3.9	2.6
64	44	February	17.7	6.7	3.3
72	50	March	22.2	10	2.5
80	57	April	26.7	13.9	1.1
90	66	May	32.2	18.9	0.7
100	74	June	37.8	23.3	0.6
104	80	July	40	26.7	2.5
102	78	August	38.9	25.6	2.7
94	70	September	34.4	21.1	1.8
82	58	October	27.8	14.4	1.4
67	46	November	19.4	7.8	1.4
58	39	December	14.4	3.9	2.2

You should check www.weather.com before you leave.

Events and Festivals

February
The Big Game (NFL Football)
Even when Las Vegas does not host the biggest game in football, sports fans (and especially sports bettors) flock to the city to place bets and watch the game on massive screens throughout the city.

Valentine's Day
There's no shortage of wedding chapels in Las Vegas. Couples exchange their vows in huge numbers on and around Valentine's Day. The city's Marriage Bureau stays open 24 hours and Elvis impersonators who officiate at many of the venues are super busy.

March

March Madness (NCAA Tournament)
Just like football's biggest event (*see above*), fans flock to see college basketball's NCAA tournament.

NASCAR
Las Vegas has become one of the top venues for auto racing. The racing season really takes off in March at The Las Vegas Motor Speedway, not too far from The Strip. www.lvms.com.

April

Great Vegas Festival of Beer
Las Vegas' premier annual food and beverage festival celebrates the best craft breweries, culinary artists, and mixologists. It's held at the downtown Las Vegas Events Center, just steps from the Fremont Street Experience. greatvegasbeer.com.

Viva Las Vegas
Slick your hair back and put on your 1950s attire at the Rockabilly Festival. The Orleans Hotel hosts greaser theme events like concerts, hot rod car show, dancing, burlesque show, pool party, and a large vendor room where you can purchase period products. www.vivalasvegas.net.

Clark County Fair & Rodeo
Las Vegas is in Clark County. The nearby community of Logandale hosts one of the nation's premier county fairs and PRCA and WPRA rodeos. Put on your cowboy hat and enjoy bull riding, barrel racing, calf roping, livestock shows, carnival rides, live entertainment, and food vendors. www.ccfair.com.

May

Electric Daisy Carnival
Nearly 500,00 people head to Las Vegas in May for the annual Electronic Dance Music (EDM) carnival featuring some of the most popular DJs and club music stars. lasvegas.electricdaisycarnival.com

June

The World Series of Poker
What's more Las Vegas than poker? This event, held in June and July, features high-stakes gamblers competing for six-figure purses. The latest venue for the tournament is Paris Las Vegas. www.wsop.com.

July/August
Independence Day
In a city known for neon lights, there's even more to illuminate the sky during the celebration of Independence Day. Phenomenal fireworks light up the valley. It's toasty in July, so there are plenty of pool parties on The Strip.

Summer Splash
It can be brutally hot in Las Vegas in the summer. Summer Splash Las Vegas can cool you off with pool parties, air-conditioned nightclubs, and some of the best DJs featuring electronic dance music. summersplashlv.com.

September
Life is Beautiful Festival
Get ready to dance and eat under the neon lights. Thousands make their way to downtown Las Vegas to listen to concerts from some of the biggest and newest bands. It's not just about music, as the festival is known for its food venues, especially those operated by celebrity chefs. www.lifeisbeautiful.com.

iHeart Radio Music Festival
Popular festival featuring performances by the biggest pop stars at the T-Mobile Arena. www.iheart.com/music-festival/.

October
Las Vegas Pride
Allies and the LGBTQ+ community come together in early October for the Pride Night Parade and Pride Festival. The Parade Main Stage is at the intersection of 4th Street and Bridger Avenue in downtown Las Vegas. The festival is held at Craig Ranch Regional Park in North Las Vegas. www.lasvegaspride.org.

Rise Lantern Festival
Head to the Mojave Desert, 25 miles (40.2 km) south of Las Vegas, in Dry Jean Lake Bed, to reflect on life. The festival has live entertainment, gourmet food, and art installments. It's known for the world's largest sky lantern release. You'll write your thoughts, dreams, and memories on a biodegradable lantern to be released into the sky, creating an incredible spectacle. risefestival.com.

When We Were Young
This nostalgic music event features iconic bands and artists from the 2000s. The popular festival, held at the Las Vegas Festival Fairgrounds, focuses on emo, punk, and alternative rock music. www.whenwewereyoungfestival.com.

November
Las Vegas Marathon
The Las Vegas Marathon is held in early November and offers three distances: a marathon (26.2 miles/42.2 km), a half marathon (13.1 miles/21.1 km), and a distance unique to the local Las Vegas area code (7.02 miles/11.3 km). The starting line is at Red Rock Canyon, and runs through downtown Summerlin, Symphony Park, 18b Arts District, Las Vegas Boulevard, and finishes at Fremont Street Experience. vegasmarathon.com.

Las Vegas Grand Prix
The Las Vegas Grand Prix is part of the Formula One World Championship. The night race is a 3.8 mile (6.1 km) race that passes some of the city's landmarks, casinos, and hotels. Speeds on the course reach up to 212 mph (341 kph). The inaugural race was held in November 2023. Formula One has signed a ten-year agreement to hold the event in Las Vegas. *Info*: www.f1lasvegasgp.com.

December
New Year's Eve
You can watch the ball drop in New York City's Times Square on television, then join nearly 500,000 revelers on The Strip, or at the downtown Fremont Experience, for a western U.S. party. Flashing neon and tremendous fireworks make for an unforgettable beginning of the year.

Insurance
Given the uncertainties in today's world, you may want to purchase trip-cancellation insurance (for coverage, check out www.insuremytrip.com). Make sure that your policy covers sickness, disasters, bankruptcy, and State Department travel restrictions and warnings. In other words, read the fine print!

Internet Access/Wi-Fi
Wi-Fi is available at most hotels, bars, cafes, and restaurants.

PLANNING YOUR TRIP/PRACTICAL MATTERS 115

Packing/Dress
Never pack prescription drugs, eyeglasses, or valuables in your checked suitcase. Carry them on. Don't ruin your trip by having to lug around bulky suitcases. Las Vegas is quite casual. It's okay to dress casually for dinner, except in more expensive restaurants.

Postal Service
An office is at 201 S. Las Vegas Blvd. #100. It's open Mon-Fri 9am-noon and 1pm-5pm. If you need a stamp, many souvenir shops sell them with postcards.

Public Transportation
The Regional Transportation Commission (www.rtcsnv.com) runs the *Deuce on The Strip* line, which is a 24-hour bus line that goes from the South Strip Transit Terminal up to the Fremont Street Experience in downtown Las Vegas. There are multiple stops along The Strip, including locations where you can connect with the Las Vegas Monorail. A single ride is $4, two hour pass $6, 24-hour pass $8, and three-day pass $20. Tickets can be purchased on the bus, at ticket vending machines, and through the rideRTC app. The Regional Transportation Commission has an extensive bus system through the greater Las Vegas area.

Smoking
Smoking is allowed in many of the hotels and casinos. Many clubs also allow smoking. No total smoking ban in Las Vegas. Smoking is prohibited in museums and on public transportation.

Tipping
Las Vegas is a tourist destination, and many workers rely on tips to make a living. Most people tip 20% at restaurants. If you are visiting from outside the United States, know that it is rare for the tip to be included in your bill.

Websites
- Made Easy Travel Guides: www.madeeasytravelguides.com
- City of Las Vegas: www.lasvegasnevada.gov/visitors
- Visit Las Vegas: www.visitlasvegas.com
- Nevada: nv.gov/visit and travelnevada.biz

6. Index

Adventuredome (Circus Circus) 24
airport 109
Allegiant Stadium 53
amusement part 24
antique shops 38
aquarium 25 (Mandalay Bay), 27 (Caesars Palace)
Area15 55
Aria 95
arrival 109
Arte Museum 26
art galleries 38
Artist's Palette (Death Valley) 78
Arts District (18b) 38
Atlantis Show 27
Atomic Golf 66
Atomic Liquors 33
Atomic Museum 25
Aviation Museum 51

Badwater Basin (Death Valley) 78
Baker, California 81
Bali Hai Golf Club 65
Bally's 98
banking 110
bars/lounges 33, 96
baseball 54
basketball, women's 53
beer festival 112
Bellagio 22, 61, 108
Bellagio Conservatory & Botanical Garden 22
Bellagio fountains 22
Big Apple Coaster 26
biking 69
birthplace of Las Vegas 47
Bodies…The Exhibition 17-18
Borax Museum (Death Valley) 75
botanical garden 22 (Bellagio), 47 (Springs Preserve), 51 (Ethel M)
brothels, legal (Pahrump) 90
buffets 108
bulldozers (Dig This) 50
bungee jumping 23
burlesque 38-39, 101
Burlesque Hall of Fame 38-39
Bus 109-110

cactus garden 51
Caesars Palace 27, 33, 61, 64, 94, 108
camping 69, 72
cannabis 110
canopy (Viva Vision) 37
Canyon Blaster 24
car racing 48
car rental 109
cars museum 29, 52
Casino (film) 33
caves (Mojave) 84
celebrity chefs 106-107
chefs, celebrity 106-107
Chinatown 104
Cima Dome (Mojave) 85
Circa Resort 39, 63, 99
Circus Circus 24, 98, 108
Cirque du Soleil 18, 100-101
CityCenter 62, 98
children, attractions/activities 42, 56
Clark County Fair & Rodeo 112
climate 111
Cold War Memorial 69
Colorado River 87, 89
Conrad (Resorts World) 93
conservatory (Bellagio) 22
Container Park 44
Cosmopolitan 64, 95, 108
Crockfords (Resorts World) 93
Cromwell 98
Crystals at CityCenter 62

Dante's View (Death Valley) 79
Davis, Sammy Jr. 32
day trips 67-90
Death Valley 74-80
Delano (Mandalay Bay) 94
Devil's Golf Course (Death Valley) 78-79
Diana, Princess 31
Dig This 50
dining 103-108
Discovery Children's Museum 42
downtown 34-44
  sleeping/hotels/resorts 99, 102
Downtown Container Park 44
Downtown Grand 102
drag brunches 59-60

INDEX 117

drag racing 48
dress 115
dunes 80 (Death Valley), 84 (Mojave)
Durango 102

Eagle Point Skywalk (Grand Canyon) 90
eating 103-108
Eiffel Tower/Eiffel Tower Experience 24
Electric Daisy Carnival 112
electronic dance music (EDM) 112
Elvis 32, 46
Elvis impersonators 46
Encore 97
Erotic Heritage Museum 28
Escape Game 27
Ethel M Cactus Garden 51
Ethel M Chocolate Factory Tour 51
Eureka Dunes (Death Valley) 80
events 111-114
Excalibur 93
excursions 67-90

fair, Clark County 112
farm 55
Fashion Show Mall 62
fees, resort 92
Ferris wheel 19
festivals 111-114
fireworks 113
Flamingo Resort 30, 92
football 53, 111
Formula One World Championship 48
Forum Shops at Caesars 27, 61
Fountains at Bellagio 22
Four Seasons (Mandalay Bay) 94
Four Queens 102
Fremont Street Experience 37
Furnace Creek (Death Valley) 74

gay 58-60, 113
Ghost Adventures (television show) 43
Gilcrease Orchard 55
GoCars Tours 110
Gold and Silver Pawn Shop 42
Golden Gate Hotel 33
Golden Nugget 99
Golden Steer 32
golfing 65-66
gondola rides (Venetian) 23
Grand Canal Shoppes (Venetian) 23, 61
Grand Canyon's West Rim 89-90
Grand Prix 48, 114

Hangover (film) 33
Harry Reid International Airport 51
haunted house 43
Henderson Silver Knights (AHL) 54
High Roller 19
hiking 69, 70, 72-73, 85
Hilton (Resorts World) 93
history (of Las Vegas) 57
hockey 53, 54
Hollywood Cars Museum 29
Hoover Dam 88-89
horses/horseback riding 69, 70
hostel 102
hotels
 downtown 99, 102
 further afield 103
 The Strip 91-99

iheart Musical Festival 113
Independence Day 113
insurance 114
Internet access 114

Joshua trees (Mojave) 85

Kelso Depot (Mojave) 83
Kelso Dunes (Mojave) 84
kids, attractions/activities 56
KISS World Mini Golf and Museum 29

Lake Mead 88-89
Las Vegas Aces (WNBA) 53
Las Vegas Aviators (MiLB) 54
Las Vegas Ballpark 54
Las Vegas Farm 55
Las Vegas Lights FC (USL) 54
Las Vegas Motor Speedway 48, 54
Las Vegas National Golf Club 66
Las Vegas Natural History Museum 43
Las Vegas North Premium Outlets 62
Las Vegas Raiders (NFL) 53
Laughlin 87
LGBTQ+ 58-60, 113
Liberace Garage 29
Life Is Beautiful Festival 113
LINQ 97
LINQ Promenade 61
Lion Habitat Ranch 49
Lou Ruvo Center 43
Luxor 16-18, 92

Madame Tussauds Wax Museum 26
Mandalay Bay Resort 25, 64, 94
maps
   Death Valley 76-77
   Downtown: Resorts 36
   Downtown: Main Sights 40
   Excursions 68
   Greater Las Vegas 7
   Mojave Desert/National Preserve 82
   Nevada 10
   Red Rock Canyon 71
   The Strip: Main Sights 12-13
   The Strip: Resorts 20-21
marathon 114
March Madness (college basketball) 112
marijuana 110
Martin, Dean 32, 33
McCarran International Airport (see
   Harry Reid International Airport)
   109
"Melting Building" 43
MGM Grand 95
MGM Park 95
Michelob ULTRA Arena 53
mini golf 29
Miracle Mile Shops 62
Mirage Resort/Volcano 31, 94
Mitchell Caverns (Mojave) 84
Mob Museum 42
mobsters 30, 42
Mojave Memorial Cross (Mojave) 85
Mojave National Preserve 82-85
money 110
monorail 110
Mount Charleston
Museum of Selfies 30
music festivals 112, 113, 114
music memorabilia 52

NASCAR 48, 54, 112
natural history museum 43
Neon Museum 35
Nevada State Museum 47
New Year's Eve 114
New York-New York 26, 93
Nobu (Caesars Palace) 94
Nomad (MGM Park) 95
Nostalgia Street Rods 52
nuclear (museum) 25

observation tower (STRAT) 23
observation wheel 19

orchard 55
organized crime 30

packing 115
Pahrump 90
Paiute tribes 57, 69
Palms 97
Paris Las Vegas 24, 94
pawn shop 42
Pawn Stars (television show) 42
Peppermill Restaurant and Fireside
   Lounge 33
petroglyphs 73
Pinball Hall of Fame 28
Planet Hollywood 93
Platinum Hotel & Spa 103
poker, World Series 112
pool scene 63-64, 113
postal service 115
pot 110
Presley, Elvis 32, 46
prices, eating 103
prices, sleeping 91
Pride Parade and Festival 113
Primm/Primm Valley 86
Princess Diana: A Tribute Exhibition 31
professional sports teams 53-54
public transportation 109, 110, 115
Pyramid at Luxor 16-17

rain 111
Rat Pack 32-33
Red Rock Canyon 70-71
Red Rock Casino, Hotel & Spa 63, 102,
   103
resort fees 92
resorts
   downtown 99, 102
   further afield 103
   The Strip 91-99
Resorts World 93
restaurants 103-108
rideshare 109
Rio Hotel and Resort 29
Rio Secco Golf Club 65
Rise Lantern Festival 113
rodeo 112
roller coaster 24, 26

Sahara 99
Salt Creek (Death Valley) 79
Santa Fe Station 102

INDEX 119

Scotty's Castle (Death Valley) 75
Selfies, Museum of 30
Seven Magic Mountains 49
Shark Reef Aquarium 25
Shelby Heritage Center 52
Shoppes at Mandalay Palace 62
shopping 23, 27, 61, 62
Showgirls (film) 33
Showgirl Sign 16
shows 100-101
Siegel, Bugsy 30, 57, 92
Signature (MGM Grand) 95
Sign, Showgirl 16
Sign, Welcome 15-16
Simmons, Gene 29
Sinatra, Frank 32, 33
skydiving 23
Skyjump (STRAT) 23
Skylofts (MGM Grand) 93
skywalk, Eagle Point (Grand Canyon) 90
smoking 115
sleeping
  downtown 99, 102
  further afield 103
  The Strip 91-99
SlotZilla (zip line) 37
soccer 54
Southshore Golf Club 66
speakeasy 42
SpeedVegas 48
speedway 48
Sphere, The 19
sportsbook/sports betting 39
sports memorabilia 52
sports teams 53-54
Spring Mountain National Recreation Area 69
Springs Preserve 47
Statue of Liberty 26
STRAT Tower 23, 97
Streisand, Barbra 33
Strip, The 14-33
  sleeping/hotels/resorts 91-99, 102-103
Summerlin 62
Summer Splash 113
swimming pools 63-64

taxis 109
temperature 111
The Professionals (film) 73
thermometer, world's largest 81

The Strip 14-33
  sleeping/hotels/resorts 91-99
tipping 115
Titanic: The Artifact Exhibition 17
T-Mobile Arena 53
Total Recall 72
tower (STRAT) 23
Town Square 61
TPC Las Vegas 66
Treasure Island 18

Ubehebe Crater (Death Valley) 79

Valentine's Day 111
Valley of Fire 72-73
Vdara 95
Vegas Golden Knights (NHL) 53
Venetian Resort 23, 61, 91
Via Bellagio 61
vintage shops 38
Viva Las Vegas 72
Viva Las Vegas Festival 112
Viva Vision canopy 37
volcano (Mirage) 31

Waldorf Astoria 95
wax museum 26
weather 111
websites 115
wedding chapels 45-46
weed 110
Welcome Signs 15-16
Welcome to Fabulous Las Vegas Sign 15
West Rim (Grand Canyon) 89-90
wheel, observation 19
When We Were Young 114
Wildlife Habitat at the Flamingo 30
Wi-Fi 114
World Series of Poker 112
Wynn 97, 108

young adults, attractions/activities 42, 56

Zak Bagans' Haunted House 43
zip line (SlotZilla) 37

Made Easy Travel Guides to Southern California

- *Palm Springs Made Easy*: Your Guide To The Coachella Valley, Joshua Tree, Hi-Desert, Salton Sea, Idyllwild, and More!

- *San Diego Made Easy*: Sights and shopping, hotels and restaurants, day trips and nightlife in "America's Finest City"

- *The Amazing California Desert*: Your guide to Joshua Tree, Hi-Desert, Salton Sea, Palm Springs, Coachella Valley, Anza-Borrego, Death Valley, Mojave Desert, and More!

- *Southern California Made Easy*: The Top Sights of Santa Barbara, Los Angeles, San Diego, Palm Springs, Joshua Tree, Mojave Desert, Death Valley, and More!

For a list of all Made Easy travel guides, and to purchase our books, visit www.madeeasytravelguides.com

Printed in Great Britain
by Amazon